RELATIONSHIP COMMUNICATION SKILLS WORKBOOK FOR COUPLES

A PROVEN GUIDE TO BUILD CLARITY, DEEPEN EMOTIONAL CONNECTION, RESOLVE CONFLICT, SET BOUNDARIES, AND BOOST RELATIONSHIP SATISFACTION

BY

MATT BROOKS

Table of Content

INTRODUCTION

> *"The single biggest problem in communication is the illusion that it has taken place."*
>
> **– George Bernard Shaw**

Do you feel like you are getting through to your partner? Seeing the same person you love so much fall out of that strong affection they used to have for you can make you question whether they still love you the way they used to.

For instance, there are times when you might have stayed at work later than usual without telling your partner a thing, then automatically assume that they would understand you had more work to do. You should also know that some partners are passive communicators. They will never tell you verbally that you did something wrong; they will act it out instead. So, how do you go about this?

Suppose you have considered why misunderstandings, conflicts, and emotional distance happen between you and your partner. In that case, it will lead you to ask yourself again: do you feel like you are getting through to your partner by communicating with them? This is because communication is one of the most essential things in a relationship, and poor communication is a one-way road to an absolute disaster.

When partners do not communicate, simple talk easily leads to arguments because they no longer recognize each other. The communication becomes aggressive, and then, sooner or later, the relationship becomes toxic and a burden.

In fact, you can only expect a relationship to last long when there is good communication. We are humans, not mind readers. Our partners or we cannot know when the other person is sad, upset, or lonely and needs companionship. I mean, how can you predict your partner's needs if you don't even talk openly?

Usually, most of us easily stumble across different tips across the internet about having the best relationships or how we can ensure that our relationship lasts forever, but how many times have we come across a tip that communication will strengthen the foundation of your partnership?

In a 2014 article published by the National Library of Medicine, communication between physicians and patients was examined, and it was found that active listening is the key to maintaining an emotional connection with your partner. If active listening — which is just one part of communication — can affect something as important as emotional connection, how effective would communication be as a whole?

Some communication problems do not even come directly from you. It is sometimes an influence from your partner's background. For example, if your partner grew up in a verbally abusive household where communication was mostly yelling at each other, it will reflect on their interactions with you. They are the kinds of people who shut down when they attempt to communicate their needs because they have a background story of being shouted at and criticized.

The truth is that every single relationship has its issues and problems. There are none without challenges. Conflicts have to arise before you can know and recognize the different needs between you and your partner, but it is up to you to ensure these conflicts are resolved and practical solutions are introduced.

However, here is the good news...you've come to the right place!

If you are still here, then it is safe to conclude that you are struggling with issues like lack of trust, conflicts and misunderstanding, emotional distance, decreased intimacy, resentment, and other related problems. Although, on the surface, these problems look unrelated, the truth is that there is one catalyst that binds them all: communication.

We can ascertain one thing: the art of effective communication must have triggered you to buy this book. Thus, since there is a general outlook on the problem(s) you are facing in your relationship, as listed above, this book will address your needs by being very clear about how the art of effective communication can help revive the declining health of your relationship. By now, you may be wondering how. Well, you'll see.

Generally, effective communication has many benefits in terms of relationship satisfaction. Several case studies have explained the advantages of communication in healthy relationships. For instance, research published by the National Library of Medicine (2021) contends that the quality of couples' communication predicts relationship satisfaction over time.

The same research further explains how positive communication patterns enhance relationship quality, whereas the accumulation of negative interactions dispels couples' satisfaction in general.

Similarly, in the Intimacy Process Model, as designed by Reis and Shaver (1988), it was foregrounded that "effective communication patterns lead to the experience of intimacy, which includes several hallmarks of a satisfying partnership such as feeling cared for, understood, and validated by one's partner."

This is not just theory. Let's go down memory lane and revise history.

Sometime in the 90s, there was the most iconic country music romance of all time: the love story of Johnny Cash and June Carter.

Their love for each other was so strong that even on June's 65th birthday, Johnny still had beautiful things to write about her. And when she finally died, he followed her just a few months later. This then begs the question, how could they retain their interest in each other for that long? Effective communication, of course! They understood what the other person needed, and were able to fit right into that need.

So, you see, learning the art of effective communication is essential. Many relationships have fallen apart because partners can't properly communicate without it, leading to conflict. And that is exactly where this book comes in.

As a result, this book will teach you how to get to your partner using the CONNECT Framework. Hence, we will teach you how to:

- Check in with yourself.
- Open your ears, eyes, and mind.
- Nurture emotional intimacy through words.
- Navigate conflict the right way.
- Equip yourself with the proper tools.
- Consciously create closeness.
- Thrive together with your partner today and every day.

Here is a sneak peek of what to expect:

- Getting to know your partner and accommodating their needs.
- Identifying your and your partner's love languages and knowing how to fulfill them.
- Showing empathy in your relationship.
- Cultivating the art of active listening and utilizing it to hear your partner out.
- Using language as an enhancement tool for emotional connection.
- Tackling conflicts through conflict resolution strategies, apologies, and forgiveness.
- Understanding emotional management techniques.
- Overcoming trust issues.

So, have you lost all hope in reviving your dying relationship? Consider this book the right surgeon you have always needed for the surgical operation. If so, let's get started!

Chapter ONE
CHECK IN WITH YOURSELF

One time, I had been worried about a presentation I wanted to give that day. It would be in front of most of the higher-ups. That had never happened before, and I needed to prove to them why I was worth my new promotion and raise. My anxiety was all for nothing, as I did incredibly well. My partner had helped prepare me, giving me tips and boosting my confidence. So, you expected me to be excited to share the news during dinner. Unfortunately, their attitude sucked out all my excitement. I was vexed. They knew how frantic I was about the presentation and how crucial it was that I did well. Why are they now disinterested? I gave up talking and went to bed, filled with resentment, which they didn't care to ask why. I slept that night believing they were in the wrong; I was in the right, waiting for an apology. I never got one.

Days passed, and things went back to normal, but I held that night against them and didn't say anything about it, writing off my partner's ability to understand. It wasn't until a week after that my partner told me that the lump found in their thyroid was not cancerous. They've been worried about a lump but were too busy to check it out. It turned out that my partner didn't tell me about finally going to the hospital about it, and didn't want to add to my anxiety about the presentation. They also kept quiet until the results were out because they feared the outcome and knew very well I was anxious in the relationship. Can you believe it? I went to bed angry that day,thinking I was in the right when, all along, my partner was worried about their life.

Thinking about it now, I realize if my partner "looked" disinterested in my excitement, something was definitely wrong. It was completely unlike them. I had failed to recognize this then. This reminds me of a story: one evening, a boy ran to his grandfather, angry that another boy had belittled him. This is what the man told the boy:

Sometimes, people make me feel sick and unempathetic about their actions. But then, I realized hate wears you down; you don't have control over what people do to you, but you do have control over how you react to it. Anger spirals into hate, and hate has too much negativity on your psychological well-being.

Think about two wolves battling it out inside you. One is white, filled with positivity, kindness, and self-control. He only fights when necessary and connects well with others. The other, black, is the opposite — angry, hateful, and quick to react. He fights anyone for any reason, his rage consuming him even though it changes nothing. Living with these wolves inside is challenging, as each fights to control my mind.

"Which wolf will win, Grandfather?" the boy asked, curious.

"The one I feed," the grandfather replied with a gentle smile.

We all have these wolves within us, battling for control. When we feed the white wolf, we nurture joy, peace, compassion, and forgiveness. This brings out our best. Feeding the black wolf, however, fills us with anger, pride, fear, and resentment, bringing out the worst in us. Eventually, it's up to us which one we nurture, as our choices shape our reactions.

These stories tell us a few things:

The enemy is within you. Your fear, anger, self-pity, sorrow, regret, ego, and other forms of negative emotion also dictate how you process and handle events.

Both wolves will always be there. You can't slay one for the other; you must learn how to live with them by turning negative emotions into positive ones.

Manage your wolves. If you decide to feed the White wolf, the Black wolf will be in the corner, waiting to attack at any opportunity of vulnerability it sees. But if it feels seen, everybody wins and stays happy. They both need each other and should be fed so that they can always be ready to fill in the roles for one another when needed.

Communication is the foundation of a strong relationship. It typically includes two or more figures, so its efficiency rests on both your inputs, not one or the other. In fact, working on your self-awareness and empathy toward understanding your emotions lays the groundwork for good communication in your relationship.

The "U" In Communicate

No matter the context, the goal of effective communication is that both parties are heard and understood. This is especially important in romantic relationships where a couple's differences can easily cause conflicts or misunderstandings. People assume communicating effectively simply means speaking and listening to others, but it goes beyond that. First, you need to understand your stance, the reason for the conversation, and its goals. This is why self-awareness is a crucial component of effective communication. That is being fully aware of your speech and its impacts. The following are a few ways self-awareness makes you a better communicator:

You become a better listener

We filter conversations through these beliefs and values. This is one reason we object to ideas and information that counter that belief. However, self-awareness allows us to better address our reception and response to information. This improves your listening skills. A good communicator typically listens attentively to the speaker without interrupting them. For instance, during a conversation about an uninteresting topic or situation, you are less inclined to *zone out* of the conversation. You will find it easy to refrain from interrupting your partner while they speak.

You receive feedback well

A self-aware person is receptive to constructive feedback. They recognize it as an avenue to become a better person. On the other hand, an individual who lacks or struggles with self-awareness might always see constructive feedback as an attack or would always internalize *all* feedback without checking if it's constructive or destructive. You can see how the former scenario would inarguably improve your relationship, as criticism between partners is quite common in many relationships.

You are more conscious of your emotions

Remember the story about the two wolves? The Black wolf is evil, filled with anger, jealousy, self-pity, etc., while the White wolf is good with all positive emotions. Only self-aware people know when they start exhibiting negative emotions and the turmoil they elicit. When you are constantly aware of your negative emotions being triggered, you are better equipped to deal with it.

For instance, you tend to react angrily whenever your partner or a friend raises their voice during conversations. Your anger tends to flare things up. Self-awareness allows you to recognize your anger triggers; this, in turn, helps you quiet such emotions, giving you the space to figure out an alternative approach to making your feelings known without escalating the situation or conflict.

So, working on yourself goes a long way to building deeper bonds with your partner, which is speared through effective communication. It allows you to fully enjoy all the benefits of communicating and ensures the longevity of that efficiency. Knowing this, it is time to begin the work by figuring out a thing or two about yourself that will help to unearth aspects of yourself that will either limit or enhance your communication abilities.

How Well Do You Know Yourself?

This quiz gives you insights into how well you know yourself and how to know yourself if you are yet to.

1. **Do you hold yourself accountable?**

    A. It is difficult not to blame other people.
    B. Yes, I owe it to me.

If your answer is A, you are rarely accountable. However, choosing B means you do the exact opposite.

2. Do you reflect on your actions?

A. It's unnecessary.
B. Yes, it makes me a better person.

Choosing B means you are introspective, which is crucial in becoming self-aware. It helps you to process thoughts and emotions. It makes you wonder why you acted a certain way.

3. Do you sit with your emotions?

A. No, I dismiss them.
B. I sit with them to figure out why I act the way I do.

If you choose B, it means you like to understand your emotions, which will help you know when you're angry, sad, or tired. It shows that you have self-awareness.

4. How do you receive feedback?

A. I feel attacked and hurt.
B. I listen attentively to feedback and use it to improve myself.

If your answer is B, it means you are aware of your weaknesses and strengths, and you are on the quest for growth and do not see everyone around you as your enemy.

5. Do you often put yourself in other people's shoes?

A. No, I don't see why I should.
B. Yes, it's very important.

If your answer is B, this means you are self-aware and empathetic. You realize people go through different things, and there's no reason to dismiss their stories.

If most of your answers are B, you have high self-awareness. The above quiz highlights the qualities of a self-aware person:

- Ability to receive feedback
- Empathy
- Responsibility

- Introspective
- Ability to understand your emotions

We've explored the significance of self-awareness when communicating with your partner and these questions to establish your current knowledge of yourself. This is the groundwork. Now, let's get down to business and break down what self-awareness is exactly, the different states it occurs, and how you can develop this aspect of yourself to build stronger and deeper bonds in your relationship.

Getting To Know You

Self-awareness is recognizing your weaknesses and strengths and regulating your behavior, emotions, and thoughts. It also means being aware of people's perceptions of you and your place in society. There are two states of self-awareness:

1. **Public self-awareness:** This revolves around how the world sees you, and it starts with societal norms that you have to adapt to to be socially accepted. While public self-awareness has many pros, like societal acceptance, we must be careful not to become victims of people's perceptions, as this could lead to anxiety about everything we choose to do or say.

2. **Private self-awareness:** This focuses more on how you see yourself internally. For instance, you're exhibiting private self-awareness when you internalize how you feel before presenting in a meeting that challenges you mentally, emotionally, and physically. This is a high level of self-awareness.

Anyone can build self-awareness regardless of age. The biggest tool you need on this journey is being intentional. That said, here are five steps to cultivating self-awareness:

- **Mindfulness**: This involves grounding your mind in the moment without getting distracted by your imagination or thoughts. When you practice mindfulness, you'll become more aware of your situation.

- **Journaling:** You can never go wrong with journaling; journaling helps you keep track of the events in your life and your reactions to each. This is possible through reflective questions like:

  - What's your favorite thing about your childhood?
  - What makes you happy?
  - What triggers your anxiety?
  - Why do you speak the way you do?
  - How was your day?
  - What would you like to do better?

  These put you in a moment of reflection — and that right there is *self-awareness.*

- **Keep a gratitude journal:** When you focus on what you are grateful for — love life, family, friends, career, or nature — you'll become more aware of the things and people that matter most to you. Know that keeping a gratitude journal differs a bit from journaling. The latter encompasses the former. However, they are directed at different effects. While journaling does lead to self-awareness, its primary purpose is to help you de-stress. A gratitude journal is your constant reminder of the many things you should be grateful for.

- **Ask for feedback**: Your loved ones' perception of you also contributes to your self-awareness. Their opinion of you exposes you to what is expected so you can avoid stepping on toes. Regardless, you will need to learn to filter their feedback. That way, you can be sure you're not leaning towards becoming a people-pleaser but a better version of yourself.

- **Accept yourself**: What's the essence of self-awareness if you cannot accept the discoveries you unearth about yourself? Understanding your emotions, strengths, and flaws is just one side. Accepting them completes your self-awareness journey.

You would have picked up on the fact that one of the aspects explored for self-awareness is understanding your emotions. Since this detail is crucial to effective communication, we need to delve deeper and consolidate our comprehension of its benefits and effects.

Adding Emotional Intelligence (EQ) to the Equation

Have you ever wondered why some people stay calm in upsetting situations that would make most people lose it? For instance, you're conversing with your date in a fancy restaurant when a waiter suddenly spills your drink all over you. No one would blame you if you got mad. In fact, it's normal to get upset in that situation. However, this may cause a scene or your emotions to spiral out of control, where you embarrass yourself and your date. There are better ways to handle this situation without causing a scene. This is where emotional intelligence comes in.

An emotionally intelligent person understands their emotions and those of others, managing them towards effective communication that could lead to conflict resolutions and an improved understanding of people. According to a paper by Jeanne Segal, a therapist and an expert in emotional intelligence, EQ connects you with your feelings and proposes actions that would lead to stronger relationships. Segal also insists that EQ is a secret to lasting relationships, as you would have built the sensitivity to take appropriate and healthy actions when dealing with your partner.

And like self-awareness, EQ also consists of several elements.

Components of EQ

Building emotional intelligence is easier said than done. You have to decide on it and make an intentional effort to build it. But what exactly are you building? There are five components of emotional intelligence. Mastering each makes you an emotionally intelligent person. They are:

- **Self-awareness**. We've spent a huge chunk of this section discussing self-awareness. Here's one reason for that. Self-awareness and emotional intelligence are relative to one another. However, when it comes to EQ, we are referring to our recognition and acceptance of the emotional part of us and how certain situations influence these feelings.
- **Self-regulation** involves the part where you manage these emotions you've become aware of. That is how often you think about actions thoroughly before you act.
- **Motivation.** External rewards like money or fame become the least of the things you are interested in. Instead, as an emotionally intelligent person, you crave internal rewards and push to fulfill inner goals and needs.
- **Empathy** is listening to people without being dismissive or judgemental. Putting yourself in others' shoes shows them compassion because you can connect to their experiences even if you haven't experienced them.
- **Social skills** involve listening and relating with people, which makes them feel welcome when conversing with you. This is fundamental to eliciting your partner's troubles or point of view towards understanding them.

When you build up these skill, you gain the the ability to understand and manage your emotions as much as those around you. This capability is a core foundation of effective communication. But why EQ? What makes these components have such an impact on building a deeper emotional connection and a long-lasting relationship with your partner?

Importance of EQ

Emotional intelligence (EQ) is foundational to building meaningful romantic relationships. When integrated with effective communication, EQ becomes a powerful tool for deepening connection, enhancing mutual understanding, and fostering intimacy. Here's how it plays a crucial role in relationships:

Conflict resolution with compassion: In any romantic relationship, conflicts are inevitable, but how they're managed can strengthen or weaken the bond. EQ allows you to approach disagreements with empathy, seeking to understand your partner's perspective without jumping to conclusions or reacting impulsively. Communicating with patience and empathy, rather than defensiveness, transforms conflict into an opportunity for growth.

Mutual growth and vulnerability: Personal growth within a relationship requires self-reflection and open communication about fears, aspirations and insecurities. Through EQ, you become more comfortable with vulnerability. Embracing vulnerability leads to a stronger, more resilient connection, allowing both partners to support each other's growth. This mutual growth strengthens and adds depth to your relationship.

Express yourself without misunderstanding: There would have been instances where you find it challenging to articulate your emotions, leading to misunderstandings or feelings of disconnection in your relationship. EQ, through self-awareness, helps you attune to your emotional cues, recognizing patterns indicating happiness, frustration, or stress. This awareness allows you to share your thoughts and feelings more confidently, avoiding further misunderstandings.

Creates a safe space for emotional honesty: Since EQ gives you the tool to have conversations without fear of misunderstanding, it transforms into a safe space for emotional honesty. You now have this fortress where you can be vulnerable and express your feelings without being judged. This prompts an improved understanding between you and your partner. While it can't be completely ruled out, you are less likely to offend your partner in this situation. As a result, conflicts are reduced, leading to a more harmonious relationship.

Strengthens intimacy and commitment: Research published in *The International Journal of Indian Psychology* supports the link between emotional intelligence and intimacy in romantic relationships. In the study, emotional intelligence positively correlated with attitudes toward intimacy and commitment. Specific aspects of EQ, such as managing emotions and understanding a partner's feelings, contributed to greater closeness and commitment. These findings highlight that emotionally intelligent individuals tend to nurture more intimate, committed relationships, as their skills in self-regulation promote deeper, lasting bonds.

EQ in romantic relationships goes beyond "good communication" and emphasizes the essence of being attuned to each other's inner worlds. When couples prioritize EQ, they build a bond based on understanding, patience, and genuine connection. These are the qualities that enable a relationship to grow and thrive. With that in mind, let's move on to four steps you can use to improve emotional intelligence.

Four Steps to Increase Your EQ

You need to reconnect with and understand your core emotions to build emotional intelligence (EQ) and develop emotional well-being. This process involves recognizing and accepting emotions as they arise rather than avoiding or suppressing them. Here are four steps to get started:

- **Observe your emotions:** Ask yourself reflective questions like: "How do I feel right now?" When you answer them, ask yourself why you feel that way and reply honestly. This way, you observe your feelings and their triggers or origins. Make this a routine; the more you observe, the better you learn about your emotions.
- **Observe your behavioral patterns**: While observing your emotions, it's important to observe your behavior, too. Study how you always act when you're stressed. For instance, you notice your partner is not showing up like they used to. Ask yourself, "How does this affect my mental and

emotional state?" This way, you'll recognize your behavioral patterns and how your emotions influence them, which will help to manage them better.

- **Identify and handle your emotions:** Labeling them as you observe them is essential. This identification leads you to come up with measures to deal with them. For instance, if you observe anger or resentment towards your partner's approach to a situation, you can now figure out ways to manage that anger or resentment. Each measure would be peculiar to the emotion felt, highlighting the importance of its identification. For example, how you manage anger will differ from resentment, sadness, or loneliness.
- **Observe and seek to understand your partner's emotions**: Now that you understand the complexity of emotions and how they impact your emotions, demanding different approaches to handling them, it's time to give others the same opportunity. While you may want to use your understanding of emotions to converse with them, you need also to learn the complexity of their feelings. Ask them questions. Probe without judging. Observe their reaction when you speak. Demand clarifications of unclear cues without aggression. Keep probing in a different context. This may seem exhausting initially... however, the reward is a more fulfilling relationship.

Like most skills, emotional intelligence takes time and practice to hone. You can start slow and take your time. Allow yourself some time to grow, and remember that things will only get better from here. Once you've mastered this, you can learn to communicate with newfound prowess.

How to Communicate with More EQ

Below are four ways you can communicate with your partner as an emotionally intelligent person:

- **Listen and acknowledge their thought process before you react:** When your partner shares an opinion you disagree with, avoid dismissing or invalidating it. Listen. After listening to your partner's opinion, you should acknowledge them before sharing yours.

- **Keep an open mind:** Couples rarely agree on everything. One person would love to have friends over; the other doesn't. While you listen to your partner's ideas, be open-minded. You don't always have to agree just to avoid conflict. Instead, find common ground where both your ideas will flourish or coexist.
- **Don't take things personally:** Avoid making it all about you whenever your partner expresses concerns. That's one way you invalidate their feelings. It's possible to receive negative feedback without getting defensive. If their approach hurts you, let them know to avoid similar occurrences in the future that would lead to conflicts.

Once you can master these, you can have conversations with your partner without having to walk around eggshells, hurt their feelings, and, most importantly, do nothing besides worsen the situation. While EQ gives you these tools, empathy would add to its depth.

Empathy

The word empathy was first introduced in 1909 by psychologist Edward B. Titchener. It was coined from the German word *einfühlung,* which means "feeling into." Empathy is your sensitivity to your partner's feelings. It is experiencing their emotions, good and bad. According to David Susman, PhD, a licensed clinical psychologist, you should do this without filtering these emotions through yours.

Research published by the *Clinical Psychopharmacology and Neuroscience Journal* suggests we achieve empathy through mirror neurons. These brain pathways activate when we experience something directly and observe someone else going through it.

A good example of a show of empathy is when your partner comes home visibly stressed after a long day, and instead of immediately sharing your big news or offering advice, you simply listen. This is empathy: you are stepping into their shoes, recognizing their feelings without judgment or trying to fix things right away. Acknowledging and understanding their emotions shows them that their experiences and feelings matter to you. This kind of response can help them feel truly seen and valued, which deepens your connection.

There are several types of empathy to learn that lead to these benefits for your relationship.

Types Of Empathy

Titchener and several other psychologists have defined empathy as being in someone else shoes. While this is the baseline, research has shown that empathy occurs in many forms. Let's explore the different types of empathy:

- **Affective empathy:** Affective empathy involves sharing in others' emotions. Consider a friend who has recently lost a loved one, for instance. If you have affective empathy, you may feel a strong sadness and sorrow when you hear the news. Because of this emotional connection, you might offer consoling words, a helping hand, or your presence when they're in need.
- **Somatic empathy**: This involves experiencing a physical reaction to others' feelings. For instance, if your partner slipped while mopping the kitchen and cried out, you might feel a pang in your chest, as if you were the one who got hurt. This bodily response can urge you to offer quick aid or comfort, such as helping them back up and getting an ice pack to help reduce any inflammation.
- **Cognitive empathy:** Unlike affective or somatic empathy, which involves feeling other people's emotions, cognitive empathy involves simply understanding how others feel. For instance, your partner has been laid off from work without warning. You can use cognitive empathy to understand their pain, figure out how they feel, even if you have never experienced that. Then, you let this knowledge guide your actions.

Recognizing the types of empathy deepens our emotional intelligence, which in turn enhances our communication, and better equips us to create stronger, more understanding relationships. Now, let's dive into why empathy is crucial and how it enriches your connection with your partner.

Significance of Empathy

Your sensitivity to your partner's emotions opens your eyes and minds to kindness. This is according to Jamil Zaki, PhD, an empathy researcher and Stanford University psychologist, who defines empathy as "a psychological superglue that connects people and undergirds cooperation and kindness" (*The Economist*, June 7, 2019). Your kindness allows your partner to feel truly heard and valued. This makes it easy for them to air their feelings and grievances and expose their vulnerability, a gigantic step towards effective communication.

Empathy also allows us to impact future situations and actions positively. Karina Schumann, PhD, a professor of social psychology at the University of Pittsburgh, says, "Empathy is a powerful predictor of things we consider to be positive behaviors that benefit society, individuals, and relationships." This allows you to make thoughtful actions and choices in the future that lead to a strong foundation of trust, enabling that deeper connection with your partner.

Empathy also prompts healthy conflict resolution. Being able to resolve conflicts is one reason why many couples push to improve their communication skills. Empathy gives you the arsenal to do so in the best way possible. This is according to Sabrina Romanoff, a licensed clinical psychologist, Professor of clinical psychology, and former clinical fellow at Harvard Medical School. Romanoff explained that, through empathetic listening, you can pick up cues and signals you may have missed that would help resolve a problem without complications.

And finally, since empathy allows us to understand other people's emotions, it can help us better relate with them. Amy Morin, psychotherapist and licensed clinical social worker, indicates that this ensures you know how, what, and what not to do, as you could essentially feel the way they do. This prevents those awkward situations where you say or do the exact opposite your partner expects of you, infuriating the already escalated situation.

While the benefit of empathy goes beyond being a better communicator, it nevertheless hugely contributes to it. However, many people aren't born empaths, and even after learning to become one, some situations can rid you of their awareness. Learn why, so you don't find yourself lacking, preventing your growth towards being more empathetic.

Why People Can Sometimes Lack Empathy

Some people lack empathy due to their nature of hyper-independence. This kind of person values self-sufficiency. You tackle problems alone and rarely lean on others. When your partner faces a difficult situation, you assume the best way to help is to give them space, thinking, "They probably want to handle it on their own, just like I would." This approach unintentionally neglects your partner's need for emotional support because you project your preference for independence onto them. Without realizing it, you have missed an opportunity to show empathy by offering comfort or simply listening.

For others, it may be due to illnesses such as autism and personality disorders like bipolar disorder, narcissistic behavior, and borderline disorder. Since people with personality disorders struggle with emotional attachment or being too needy, it may prevent such individuals from being empathetic.

The good news is that you can develop empathy regardless of any psychological barriers. It may not be a walk in the park, but with more effort, you can become sensitive to your partner's feelings.

Ways to Improve Empathy Towards Effective Communication

There are measures you can take to be more empathetic during conversations with your partner that lead to better communication and stronger bonds. Susman suggests some ways:

- **Engage with curiosity and openness**: Start conversations with your partner, inviting them to share their thoughts and feelings freely. Approach each topic with genuine curiosity, asking questions that help you see things from their perspective.
- **Tune into nonverbal cues**: In relationships, emotions are often communicated through body language, tone of voice, and subtle mood shifts. Notice if their tone changes, they hesitate, or seem tense about certain topics. Recognizing these cues helps you respond to their needs even when not directly expressed.
- **Take thoughtful actions**: Empathy goes beyond understanding — it's about showing you care through meaningful actions. Accept that even small gestures can make a big difference in your partner's life. Acknowledge their needs by doing something thoughtful, like preparing their favorite meal when they've had a tough day, offering a listening ear, or leaving a supportive note. Now, while these actions don't scream empathy, they are intentional acts that would show them they're valued, reinforcing that you're attentive to their well-being.
- **Use empathetic statements**: Just as it is possible for some to sometimes lack empathy, certain situations may rid you of your ability to show empathy even when you've developed such. For instance, you could have had a rough day or find it truly challenging to listen to your partner due to their attitude. In both these scenarios, being unempathetic doesn't help. This is where using empathetic statements

comes in. They are expressions you can easily adopt in conversations when you have no clue what to say. Here are some empathetic statements to give you a headstart:

- I'm so sorry you're going through all this.
- I can imagine how you must be feeling.
- I'll always be here for you if you need my help.
- How can I be there for you?
- You don't have to do this alone, so let's get some help.
- I'm here for you.
- Your emotions are valid.
- I am proud of the woman/man you have become.
- I appreciate you not letting what you went through define you.
- Thank you for sharing this with me; it means a lot.

Interactive Element

You've understood the significance of self-awareness, emotional intelligence, and empathy. Now, it's time to get to work. This section is designed to help you better understand your emotions and attitudes. Let's start with 25 prompts to help you become a highly emotional, intelligent partner. They also come with step-by-step instructions on how to embrace self-awareness throughout the process:

1. What sort of conversation do I hate to have?
2. What sort of conversation would I like to have?
3. Who do I become when I'm in a relationship?
4. What is that relationship experience that made me a better version of myself?
5. How do I know I've fallen in love with someone?
6. What's my favorite thing to do with my partner?
7. How do I know when to leave a relationship?
8. What type of conversation makes me feel uncomfortable?
9. What gives me triggers?
10. Why am I dismissive?
11. Why do I run from conversations?

12. Why am I so emotional?
13. What do I need to change about myself?
14. Why do my friends and significant other say I lack empathy?
15. Why do people say I could be a bit judgemental?
16. What qualities attracted me to my partner?
17. Why does my partner's silence bother me?
18. Why does my partner think I'm insecure?
19. Why do I care about this person so much?
20. Why do I feel this way when my partner gives me negative feedback?
21. Why did my partner say I felt attacked when called out?
22. How does my partner perceive me?
23. What does a healthy relationship mean to me?
24. What do I love the most about my friends?
25. What does family mean to me?

To become emotionally intelligent, you must first be aware of yourself. Here is an exercise that will help you learn more about yourself:

1. Who are you?

As simple as this sounds, it's a reflective question. You have to ask yourself who you are repeatedly until you've internalized it. The more you ask, the more it peels off the multiple layers of your identity. You could have someone ask you if it's comfortable with you. Is your identity tied to what you do or your relationship status? Is it tied to what your parents want you to be? Who *are* you? What is your identity tied to? Who do you want to be before the world tells you who to be? Understanding your identity is a great way to start understanding yourself.

2. The Three Whys

This exercise is used to know the reason behind a problem. It was developed by Sakichi Toyoda and was used by Toyota to evolve its manufacturing process. When you ask the first "why," you will always have a quick response; you may not have to think of it before it slips out of your mouth. It becomes challenging to ask the second "why" and the third "why." It might make you feel like you don't know what you're doing, which clarifies why you do what you do. You can ask a friend to help you to make this more fun.

This exercise clarifies who you are and why you are here. You can also use it to gain clarity when you are confused. It makes you know why you are here.

3. Record your ABCs

This idea is based on the ideology that external events (A) do not cause emotions (C), but our beliefs (B) do. Albert Ellis's ABC is essential to his rational-emotive behavior therapy (REBT), which preceded cognitive behavioral therapy (CBT).

Recording your ABCs will give you a reflection on why you act the way you do after events so you can be better at handling such events when they happen again. This means recording the following:

- Activating events that trigger your inner dialogues
- Beliefs you formed after the events
- Consequences of the events or how you feel

This exercise will help you understand how you handle stress. Imagine you planned a date night with your partner, and they kept you waiting for hours. It might piss you off and make you start passing aggression to people around you. Instead, you can take a deep breath in and out, relax your mind, and focus on what you can control. You can call them to ask why they have not shown up or if they'd like to rain check. This exercise teaches us how to handle adverse situations and turn them into positive ones, not the other way around when negative emotions make a mess out of us.

4. Johari Window

This exercise focuses on understanding what we know and don't know about ourselves.

It's divided into four regions:

Blindspot: This region features things about yourself that others know but you don't. Your skills and talents can be a blindspot, especially if you struggle with imposter syndrome. That's why receiving feedback is so important; it helps you appreciate yourself more.

Arena: This area features what both you and others know about you. It gives you more clarity on who you see yourself as.

Facade: This is a side of yourself you are aware of but not others, usually because you don't feel comfortable sharing this part of yourself with people.

Unknown self: This region features things about you that are unknown to you and others.

You can ask your loved ones for feedback about yourself and ask them to describe you in three ways. Be open to negative and positive responses and consider any feedback you get. Now, this is where self-awareness comes in. If you know yourself enough, some things might be familiar. It will also help you determine what is true because you don't have to do everything others suggest you do.

5. The Wheel of Life

This tool helps you increase awareness in eight critical areas: career, finances, health, friends and family, romance, personal development, fun and recreation, and physical environment.

Here's how to go about it:

- Draw a circle using paper and pencil, and divide the circle into eight equal parts according to the above categories. The result will be a pie chart.
- Rate your level of satisfaction on a scale of one to ten. Do this with your gut, and be sure of what you want.
- Shade each segment to represent your level of satisfaction. You can use different colors to highlight each area. Consider asking reflective questions like these to determine how you shade each segment.

- **Career:** Are you fulfilled? What would you like to change about your career?
- **Finances:** What is your current net worth? Do you stick to your monthly budget plan?
- **Romance:** Are you happy in this relationship? Do you see a future with your current partner?
- **Health:** Do you take care of yourself? How is your state of mind?
- **Friends and family:** How do you feel when you spend time with them? Is your support system helpful?
- **Personal development:** What are you feeding your mind and your soul? What's your priority right now?
- **Physical environment:** Are you taking care of your environment? Is your environment healthy?

- Now, examine the wheel, and you'll see your levels of satisfaction; the areas you are least and most satisfied with. You can now see the object of dissatisfaction and work to turn your fortune around, channeling your effort into the right areas.

This chapter lays the groundwork for effective communication and deeper emotional connections with your partner by emphasizing the importance of self-awareness, empathy, and a profound understanding of your emotions. Cultivating these qualities prepares you to engage in more meaningful interactions. However, many people mistakenly believe communication is solely about expressing the right words. It's not! The next chapter will shift our focus to an often-overlooked aspect of communication: active listening. You'll discover how truly hearing your partner fosters a deeper understanding between you.

Chapter

TWO

O: OPEN YOUR EARS, YOUR EYES, AND YOUR MIND

> "
>
> *"We have two ears and one mouth so that we can listen twice as much as we speak."*
>
> **— Epictetus**

Tiffany and Nathan were a young couple who lived in a quiet town. They were deeply in love with each other but had very different personalities. Tiffany was full of life and energy and never hesitated to express her feelings, while Nathan was quieter, preferring to listen, think, and choose his words carefully before speaking.

One evening, after a long day, the couple got home, and Tiffany seemed stressed and absent-minded. Nathan noticed her gazing into the distance and tapped her gently. "Babe, what's going on with you?" he said. "You've been quiet since you got back from work. What's on your mind?" Tiffany snapped back into reality. She tried to explain that she was upset about her job, but the words wouldn't form. When they finally did, they got tangled, and Nathan listened quietly as she expressed how she felt.

Tiffany noticed Nathan hadn't said anything while she talked and got irritated.

"Did you hear what I said? Why are you so quiet?"

Nathan took her hand and led her to sit beside him. "I heard you, honey," he said softly. "But sometimes, I think it's better to hear you out before responding. I want to know what got you so worked up."

Hearing his response, Tiffany took a deep breath and felt her nerves calming down. She realized she needed someone to listen rather than talk to her.

"Thank you," she said. "I had no idea how badly I needed to let everything out."

Silence filled the room, and Tiffany felt more at peace than she had in days. After some time, Nathan spoke up, suggesting thoughtful ideas and making comments that resonated with what she had shared. Even though he didn't have perfect answers for all of her problems, she could tell he understood her by how he spoke.

From that night on, Tiffany and Nathan's relationship became more balanced, and they learned to value each other's strengths. Nathan showed her that listening wasn't just about hearing words; it was about connecting to someone's emotions through their words.

"We have two ears and one mouth to listen twice as much as we speak," Nathan had once said, and Tiffany thought of this quote as he wrapped her in his arms. She smiled as she realized how true it was. Listening had become a message between them that strengthened their love.

Have you ever had a friend or partner talk to you, only to respond and hear them say, "You're not listening to me." What if they were right? Someone would only say that if you say something different from what they want to hear or when you keep interrupting them. Listening to people express themselves will make them feel heard and understood and see you as a safe space. According to research by the University of Illinois, when people feel heard and understood, they are more likely to trust and feel connected to those they are communicating with.

In this chapter, we will explore an often overlooked but fundamental aspect of communication — one that involves little to no speaking at all: active listening.

Facts About Listening

Listening is receiving, interpreting, and understanding spoken words with full attention and empathy. You can't build a close relationship with someone unless you know them. And to understand what someone is saying, you need to listen to them and figure out what they mean before airing your opinion.

Listening to someone doesn't mean nodding and waiting for them to finish talking so you can respond. Instead, it's about giving your undivided attention by showing you care about the person talking to you.

According to research, a part of our brain called the prefrontal cortex is responsible for such things as memory, emotions, impulse control, problem-solving, social interaction, and motor function. It is also active when we pay attention to someone by being mindful of what they say.

Research also shows that women listen with both temporal lobes, while men use just one to listen. This may be why your significant other often seems absent-minded when you talk to them. There's a longstanding idea that men are more forgetful than women, and this research suggests that it could be because of how their brains are wired.

Our ears work faster than our mouths, regardless of gender. This means we can process spoken words faster than we can articulate them. Humans can listen at an impressive rate of about 459 words per minute, which is faster than the rate at which most people speak; an average speaking rate is about 125–175 words per minute.

A study from the University of California, Berkeley, discovered that when people listen to someone recount a personal story, their brain activity synchronizes with that of the storyteller. This is known as "neural mirroring." It lets people understand the story by reflecting the speaker's mind and letting them experience and feel what the speaker is feeling. This helps people understand each other better, feel connected, and have compassion for each other.

We all listen effortlessly every day, which makes it easy for us to think we have what it takes to be labeled a good listener. But few of us actually are. The average person yet to develop their listening skill has about 50% retention of any conversation, and that's only right after the conversation; forty-eight hours later, average retention drops to nothing less than 25%.

So, what's the point of all of these interesting facts about listening?

The Importance of Listening

Good listening skills can help you understand your partner's needs and feelings, which makes listening an essential part of communication. Communication problems are one of the leading causes of most relationship issues, and you can build a healthy relationship by working on your communication skills. Let's look at some ways listening can benefit your relationship.

1. It reduces misunderstandings

Listening to your partner when communicating with you prompts you to ask them questions to be sure you heard them right and saves you the mental stress of overthinking. I used to be with someone who always said, "If there's something you don't understand, please ask questions." That became my mantra ever since.

You can only provide feedback to your partner when you listen to them. The purpose of feedback is to signal that you're listening to them. You can do this verbally or nonverbally. For example, you can say "You're right" or "Right" for verbal feedback. At the same time, you maintain eye contact or nod your head for non-verbal feedback. This way, you will build trust between you and your partner.

2. It builds intimacy

When you take the time to listen to your partner, you get to know them better and what matters to them, which strengthens your bond. If you practice active listening with your partner, you will be their go-to person whenever they need to talk about anything that makes them happy or worried. However, if you come off as a bad listener, you'll only make them find someone else to confide in. To maintain intimacy with your partner, you must make them know you are always there to listen. And it's not enough to tell them this; you must also show it in your actions.

3. It shows that you care

Your partner might feel hurt when they realize you aren't listening to them. It makes them think you don't care about what they are talking about as much as they care to listen to you. You might give them excuses for why you aren't paying attention, but it won't change their mind when it becomes a pattern. On the contrary, listening to them shows you care about them and everything else. It shows they have your undivided attention. Listening to your partner is a great way to show they mean a lot to you, which is important in building a successful relationship.

Even if you are a terrible listener, you can improve your listening skills if you work. The following section teaches how to do this.

What's Your Listening Style?

There are different listening styles for various conversations. Good communicators know how to adapt to the best listening style that fits the situation of the conversation they are in. In this section, we will explore the listening styles in detail:

People-Oriented Listening

People with this listening style are often concerned about the emotional well-being of others to offer emotional support. They are usually supportive, understanding, and caring. People-oriented listening style is more valuable in interpersonal communication because it creates a safe space for vulnerability without the fear of being judged or mocked. People with this listening style are empathetic and are most likely in professions such as counseling, social work, or nursing. People often consider empathy feminine, so more women are empathetic than men.

For example, your partner comes home stressed and vents about their toxic work environment. You could respond, "I'm so sorry about your work environment. I understand you don't feel safe. A toxic work environment can be draining and make you less productive. How are you feeling now?" This is an empathetic and compassionate response, typical of a people-oriented listener character.

Action-Oriented Listening

People with this listening style focus on what action needs to be taken based on what has been communicated to them and try to initiate it. They get frustrated at disorganization because it distracts them from getting things done. Action-oriented listening is effective when something needs to be done about the issue on the ground. In the example I gave in the previous listening style, an action-oriented listener would say, "What do you want to do now? Did you tell your boss how this makes you feel? You should figure something out." Action-oriented listeners differ from people-oriented listeners in that while they may not connect with you emotionally, they can help you take action.

Content-Oriented Listening

Content-oriented listeners must have information about something and process it before deciding and acting on it. They constantly evaluate and analyze the information they receive. They are judges and are often found in academic fields such as social sciences, sciences, and humanities. Politicians and content-oriented listeners will want to hear the parties involved in an argument before making peace. At times, they might even challenge the conflicting parties to see things from each other's point of view.

Time-Oriented Listening

Time-oriented listeners are usually efficient with their time. They want you to get to the point while checking in to be sure they get their appointment done while you move on to the next thing on your to-do list. They might interrupt you and avoid eye contact because they must keep things going, not because they don't care about or listen to you. Professionals with this listening style include medical personnel, event planners, project managers, executive assistants, freelancers, content creators, etc.

Knowing your listening style and that of your partner will help you figure out how to communicate with them and understand their reactions to what you are saying. Now that you know your listening style, let's consider what makes you a good listener.

What Makes You a Good Listener?

Listening and hearing are different. Hearing is passively listening to a sound without focusing your attention on it. For instance, you might passively hear music, the waves of the ocean, or the sound of a baby crying while doing an activity without paying attention. On the other hand, listening requires intentional effort; it requires your undivided attention, as you must understand the message in a person's spoken words and recollect and relay it. So, what are the traits of a good listener?

A good listener is always in the present.

They give their full attention to the speaker, cutting off all distractions, avoiding the temptation to multitask, and making the moment about the speaker. Staying present this way takes a lot of work. Focusing your mind and attention on one person could be difficult, but you can do it with self-awareness. I'll recommend you practice mindfulness.

They are open-minded.

A good listener avoids judging the speaker; instead, they focus on what the speaker communicates verbally and through their body language. It's so easy to be close-minded that becoming open-minded takes deliberate effort.

They are patient.

Being a good listener requires patience, which includes listening to the speaker without interrupting them. Sometimes, you might be tempted to say something like: "I can relate to that, too" or "Your experience is nothing compared to mine" while the person is talking. But it would help if you weren't competing with someone else's experiences.

It's better to summarize or paraphrase the conversation to let the speaker confirm if you heard them right. This reassures them that you're listening to them. But don't do this while the speaker is still talking. Instead, wait for the speaker to give you a break before you come in.

A good listener asks questions.

In listening, it is important to show that you're engaged in the conversation. So, don't hesitate to ask thoughtful questions. This shows the speaker that you're making an effort to understand them. When you ask the right questions, you'll understand the speaker more clearly, making the conversation smoother and less stressful.

Barriers to Listening

If you think you lack one or more of the qualities listed above, don't worry. There's time to learn and practice them, but it's best to know the common listening barriers to learn how to tackle them and improve. Listening barriers may be emotional, psychological, or natural; sometimes, they could be physical and environmental. Let's explore each in more detail and determine which is yours.

Physical barriers are the most apparent listening barrier. Anything that causes discomfort to your well-being can make it difficult for you to listen, such as noise, dogs barking, vehicles, or even the distance between the speaker and you, the listener.

Environmental factors can also make it hard to listen attentively. For instance, if the temperature is too hot or cold or the area is too dark or unsafe, you might feel uncomfortable, affecting your focus.

Psychological reasons such as anxiety, stress, and worrying can also hinder active listening. For example, someone who is going through stress from work and hasn't had adequate sleep for a while now might find it hard to concentrate, let alone listen to someone speak.

A language barrier can also hinder listening. This happens when the speaker and listener are from different cultures and communicate in other languages they can't understand. The purpose of communication is to be understood, but this can be difficult or even impossible when there's a language barrier.

How to Overcome Listening Barriers

The first step to overcoming a listening barrier is to know precisely what the barrier is; this way, you'll know what to work on. For instance, if your barrier is affected by physical factors, it is ineffective to solve it through psychological solutions. This is why you need to identify precisely what your barrier is.

If your barrier comes through environmental factors, you can help yourself by creating a comfortable environment. It means you have to reduce the noises, manage the ones you can't control, and brighten the room to make it conducive.

You can use microphones and speakers in an auditorium to ensure everyone hears the speaker well enough. Use eye contact, nod, and give feedback to indicate your understanding. Ask questions if needed to show your level of involvement.

If your barrier is psychological, you can manage it by developing empathy and asking for breaks. When you have shown your partner that you understand your perspective, it allows them to understand you when you request a break from them. Besides, rest prevents fatigue and helps maintain concentration levels between you and your partner.

Lastly, if your barrier emerges through a physical factor, you can help yourself by minimizing distracting objects or situations surrounding you. This may include finding quiet environments to converse or improving the physical acoustics around you, such as using adequate lighting and providing comfortable seating.

Active Listening

Active listening involves listening to someone with your full attention. It goes beyond just hearing the words; it means listening attentively to someone without interrupting them. To practice active listening, you should focus solely on what the person communicates verbally and non-verbally instead of interrupting them or thinking of what to say next. When you focus on what the person is saying, you subconsciously build good listening skills. Trying to respond to the person while they are talking could make you miss the point and make them think you don't understand them.

Active listening is listening to understand. When two people are conversing, there are two things to look out for in the message and the attitude. First, they focus on how the message is relayed and look for non-verbal cues, like the speaker's body language, tone of voice, and facial expressions. Non-verbal cues often convey deeper information that the speaker might not express verbally. Also, active listeners tend to take their time to listen to others express their feelings before responding to them. This makes the speaker feel heard and cared for.

Importance of Active Listening

Active listening varies with each person. While some are naturally more skilled at it, others must practice it daily due to the nature of their jobs. These include hairdressers, barbers, photographers, teachers, gym instructors, dieticians, and therapists. Whatever you do, active listening is valuable in our personal and professional relationships, even in conversations with strangers.

Another benefit of active listening is that it promotes empathy. Everyone has empathy at varying levels; it's like a muscle you can develop if you put in the work. If you don't use it, it can lead to atrophy, but overusing it can lead to empathy fatigue. When you practice active listening, connecting to other people emotionally, physically, or mentally becomes more accessible, which will help you build close relationships and communicate more effectively with clients.

When you develop an interest in someone's thoughts and feelings, you show that you value them, which makes them feel validated. Mutual respect builds self-confidence and healthy boundaries.

Conflict is a natural, inevitable part of any relationship. Active listening is essential in those moments because it makes you listen to what the other person is saying. It opens you up to having tough conversations, leading to an agreement to settle conflicts.

Active Listening Techniques

In this section, I share some active listening techniques to help you listen attentively and communicate more effectively. Practice them regularly so they feel natural with time, but remember that they are not a checklist but simply a guide.

The first active listening technique worth exploring is **paraphrasing**. Paraphrasing the speaker's words shows you're genuinely interested in what the speaker is saying and encourages them to keep talking. To paraphrase, you only need to repeat the speaker's words in your own words. For instance, when your partner says, "I am so stressed out from work today," you could paraphrase by saying, "Did you say you are exhausted due to work stress?"

Another effective method is to verbalize the speaker's emotions. It conveys a message to the speaker that you understand and helps them assess their feelings. Some partners don't know how to express their emotions in words, but you can see it from their actions or underlying words. Once you catch the whiff, you can help them verbalize their feelings by asking them, "You look sad. Are you fine?"

You may also ask thoughtful questions to get more information, like "How does that make you feel?" and "How else do you think it should be done?" Besides helping you gather more information, asking questions can encourage the speaker to keep talking because they'll know you're invested in what they're saying.

Summarizing the speaker's message to follow up on the conversation and gather more information also creates room for more discussion.

Clarify the speaker's words to help them see things from another point of view. Create a wrong interpretation to get more explanations. For example, you may say, "Did you call to apologize that same day?"

You could be more curious about your partner to get more information; you can achieve this by asking questions. For example, did you handle the situation well enough?

These techniques will help you improve your active listening skills. Remember, listening requires conscious effort. In the next section, you'll learn the meanings behind common body language, facial expressions, and non-verbal cues.

The Art of Non-Verbal Communication: Body Language, Facial Expression and Non-Verbal Cues

Since I learned how important face-to-face communication is, I stopped discussing important details that carry emotional tones through texts or phone calls. A friend once shared a little disagreement with his wife, which they didn't resolve before he left for work that day. His wife later realized she was wrong and called to apologize while he was in a meeting.

Without holding any grudges, my friend responded with an "okay" and dropped the call. But the result was that she thought he was still angry at her when he was only busy. This shows how important nonverbal communication is. His wife thought he was still angry because even when she heard him say it was OK, his bland tone suggested otherwise.

Most couples think communication ends with speech, but it doesn't. Experts believe speech accounts for just 30% of communication. There are extra overlays to communication that add depth to effective communication, which is the art of non-verbal communication.

What Is Non-Verbal Communication?

There are primarily two branches of communication — verbal and non-verbal. While the verbal is often capitalized on, the non-verbal makes sure we don't get misinterpreted. Body language, facial expressions, and non-verbal cues help make our speeches much more straightforward. For instance, it's hard to believe someone who tells you they are OK while wearing a gloomy face. It doesn't work that way. This means the mouth can be saying one thing while the body is saying something entirely different. This is why the art of non-verbal communication is necessary. However, mastering non-verbal communication starts with familiarizing yourself with its modes:

1. Body language

Body language is the way we communicate with our body. We often convey a message to our partners through body language without even being conscious. Simple body gestures such as reclining in the middle of a conversation can signal to your partner that you are tired of listening to them and want to leave. Likewise, yawning constantly when talking to someone is sending them a mental signal that you are bored and uninterested in what they have to say and that they should keep quiet.

Body language is as inexhaustible as the meanings to them. Smiling, too, is body language. As an intentional communicator, you need to embrace the Duchenne smile more. This is the kind of smile where you pull up the corners of your mouth while squinting your eyes. It makes you look more approachable and friendly.

Tilting your head to one side is another example of body language. When you tilt your head during a conversation, it signals to your partner that you are listening and engrossed in what they say. People want to feel heard and valued, so this is one of the most recommended body language.

2. Facial expression

The face is another medium that expresses non-verbal communication. Sometimes, the expression on a person's face can help us determine whether we can trust what they're saying or just lie. For instance, when I said earlier that it's hard to believe someone who claims they're doing fine while having a gloomy look on their face, it's because of their facial expression.

A study found that the most trustworthy facial expression involves raising the eyebrows slightly and smiling. Researcher Paul Ekman also supported the universality of a diverse facial expression tied to emotional outputs such as joy, anger, fear, surprise, and sadness.

3. Non-verbal cues

As the name implies, non-verbal cues exclude verbal communication (words). They are straightforward, and it is easy to discern their meanings. Maintaining eye contact with your partner during a conversation can be an excellent way to lay emphasis and show seriousness. In context, imagine telling your partner how much you love them while looking directly into their face or away. Which one is more believable? The former, of course!

You've done so much learning all along, wading through such important things as active learning, identifying your learning styles, and the art of non-verbal communication. Now, let's get more practical with all we have learned.

Interactive Element

Are You Really Listening?

Judging by how far we have come, it would be a total waste of time if I didn't explain how important listening to your partner is. And when I say listening, I mean active listening. So, the big question is whether you are really listening to your partner or just hearing them. As much as both options read the same, they are two different things: while you listen to absorb, you hear to respond. However, the progress of a successful relationship is more about how much of your partners' needs you have absorbed into your day-to-day activities than how often you have told them you have heard them. So, how do you show your partner you are really listening?

Ask your partners these questions:

1. **How can it be better?** This question lets them engage you with their viewpoint and further stretch the conversation.
2. **Can I know more about that?** Sometimes, you might think you totally understand your partner's spoken *and* unspoken words when you don't. You can give them the room to explain themselves by asking this simple question. Trust me, it works in all situations.
3. **How can I help?** You may put yourself in someone else's shoes only to realize your foot sizes differ. This means that no matter how much you try to relate to your partner's problem, you will only sometimes know what they need. So, ask them and let them tell you what specific help they may need. That way, they can appreciate confiding in you.
4. **You said x, am I correct?** This is your way of repeating what they have said to be sure you understand and are getting everything.
5. **What do you think is the way forward?** Asking this question is signaling to your partner that you are willing and open to solutions. It's an excellent question to always ask your partner in a conversation, especially about a conflict or an issue.

Once you have confirmed that you have listened to your partner effectively, there is one more step to go. Just as your partner has had to answer some questions, you have some to answer, too.

Three questions to ask yourself:

1. Do I really understand what they mean?
2. What are their non-verbal signals saying to me?
3. How do I support them?

Asking yourself these questions will narrow down three things:

- First, that you are not misinterpreting what is coming out of their mouths, and it also helps you direct the focus of your understanding.
- Second, that you can read beyond what they are saying.
- Third, that you are always willing to help and support your partner in the ways they need it.

If you can't answer these three questions, refer to the five questions above.

Are You a Good Listener?

It is not enough to understand every situation in this section. There is a need to make sure you assess yourself personally to see how much you are improving your listening skills. To do this, I've prepared an assessment test for you. The guide is pretty simple. All you need to do is rate yourself in the following situations and total your score at the end of the assessment using the figures below as a guide.

Very often = 5, often = 4, occasionally = 3, seldomly = 2, and once in a while = 1.

____ I listen even when I'm not interested in the conversation.

____ I am open to new ideas that don't conform to mine.

____ I maintain eye contact when listening to my partner.

____ I ensure I'm not defensive when being blamed.

____ I try to recognize the unspoken emotions in my partner's words.

____ I listen without passing judgment or pushing criticism.

____ I don't allow myself to get distracted when being spoken to.

____ I avoid jumping to conclusions.

____ I listen for more than the things I just want to hear.

____ I don't avoid complex topics or conversations with my partner.

____ I am willing to proffer help and support.

____ I discern the meanings of the non-verbal cues I notice.

____ I focus more on what is being said rather than make assumptions.

Scoring metrics:

100–75: you are an active listener! Keep it up.

74–50: you are almost there. Keep pushing it.

49–20: listening isn't your forte; start paying attention to the details we discussed earlier.

I'm Here . . . I Hear

Communication is vital in every relationship, so listening is more important than speaking. When you listen, you get to absorb the emotional needs of the person speaking and determine how to fit your actions into their interests without necessarily compromising yours. It also signals that you are there with them and hear them. Thus, if you are unsure what exercises to complete concerning active listening, you could take the ones below.

1. Fireside chats

When you think of fireside chats, picture a date without the fancy dresses and fancy restaurants. You set the mood for romance but not as exaggerated as a date. You should pick a cozy place where you are sure you will not be interrupted during your conversation, then, if the weather allows you to, light a fire. Suppose it doesn't; be creative and use a few candles, three or four drops of lavender essential oil in your diffuser, and a hot cup of cocoa or tea to set the mood. You should set a timer afterward, and then you should just talk. It doesn't have to be serious; just chat and connect with them.

2. Emotional charades

As I mentioned earlier, just because you can fit yourself in someone else's shoes doesn't mean the shoes will fit you. Most times, miscommunication happens during conversations because we tend to read meaning into things. It is like when you and your partner are standing between a number of six or nine. For one of you, the number is six, but for the other, the number is nine. Neither is wrong here; it is just the perspective with which the individual views things. Hence, to ensure you understand your partner well, you can key into a game of charades where you perform how you act, probably when you are happy or sad, and let them interpret it.

3. Couples' telephone

If you remember the game or telephone we used to play when we were little, where we'd whisper a message into one person's ear and repeat it among one another till it gets to the last person, then you should understand this quickly. Set a time for each other — like thirty seconds or a minute. Then the other partner should communicate anything while you repeat what they said. The sense of it is simple. If you can't repeat what they said within just thirty seconds, how can you be certain you heard them correctly when they talked at length with you? The key is, therefore, to exercise patience when communicating with them.

Active Listening Exercises for Healthy Communication

There are some senses that some of us are born with: smell, sight, touch, taste, and hearing. However, we can sharpen each of these things. For instance, when you find the right teacher, you will learn how hearing can become listening when done with intentionality. And since you have found just the right teacher, what active listening exercises could you engage in to foster healthy communication?

Reflective listening: Whenever you and your partner are discussing, always find a way to paraphrase what they have said to make sure you understand them. This is an inward reflection for an outward result.

Extended eye contact exercises: This might sound far-fetched, but by simply looking into your partner's eyes for a while as they speak — say five minutes — without saying a thing, you are sending them a mental message that they have your attention. This makes them open up to you even better.

Mirroring exercise: Reflection, validation, and resolution are three reasons for this exercise. These are the practical steps to it:

—X: when you did (something), it made me feel (emotion). This can be concise and kept simple. For example, "When you don't tell me you love me, it makes me feel unloved."

—Y: You mean that when I did (something), it made you feel (emotion). Is that correct? **If you can't repeat exactly what they said, try your maximum effort first. It would help if you didn't try to interpret or use your own words.**

—if Partner Y says it correctly, Partner X should say "yes." If not, Partner X should repeat the original statement.

— Y: Is there more?

— If partner X has more to share, they should repeat the step from above again. If not, partner X should say "No, that's all."

This chapter explored the common belief that communication is primarily about saying the right things. But we dived deeper into what contributes to effective communication: active listening. I have established the difference between hearing and listening by explaining the importance of genuine listening. However, it is not enough to listen to your partner; you must also know how to communicate with them intimately. The next chapter will, therefore, explore the various ways to nurture emotional intimacy through what is popularly called love language.

Chapter THREE

N: NURTURE EMOTIONAL INTIMACY THROUGH WORDS

"

"The words you speak become the house you live in."

— Hafiz

In a neuroscience experiment titled "Do Words Hurt," Maria Richter and some collaborating scientists monitored the brain responses of certain subjects to auditory and imagined negative words. During the process, they found out how painful or damaging words increase implicit processing (IMP) within the subgenual anterior cingulate cortex (sACC) — negative words tend to release stress and anxiety-inducing hormones. That's a lot of science jargon, but what's the takeaway?

No matter how insignificant you think words are, they tend to affect you. In fact, you are naturally influenced by the words others say to you. If you are in a bad mood, simple, encouraging words have enough power to make you feel good again. Likewise, if you are in a good mood, words of discouragement can easily rid you of your last drop of happiness.

Usually, most people tend to believe that the only way to express love is by acting it out. So, if you want to show your partner how much love you have for them, you buy them cars or houses, take them on dates in expensive restaurants, or even take them out on a vacation to the Maldives. This is an excellent way to show affection, but there are other ways. Actions that aren't backed with words are like a pizza without toppings. Even though the main ingredient is right there, what is the beauty of it?

To help you understand better, I'll share this story about a couple who have been married for over fifty years. When asked how they managed to sustain their love and marriage for that long, the husband smiled and said, "Every morning, I always tell her I love her. And it is not just because I do, but because I know it plants something in her heart that keeps blooming all day."

Here, the man's simple, intentional act of saying romantic words to his wife created a strong foundation to keep them together for over fifty years. It wasn't just about how many cars, roses, or diamond necklaces he had bought for her. Instead, it was the affirming words he shared every day that strengthened their bond over time. This shows that words are like the bricks with which an emotional home is built. It could either build it up or tear it down, depending on how they are used. In summary, strengthening an emotional connection can fall on the shoulders of words, and we'll explore how in the next section.

How Words Affect Emotional Connection

There are two major religions in the world: Christianity and Islam. Now, in a chapter in the Bible, it was written that the earth was without form and void after its creation until God said, "Let there be light," and there was light. Similarly, a chapter in the Qur'ān states that whenever Allah intends a thing, "He will say to it, 'Be!' and it is."

Beyond religion, the main point of these examples is that words hold so much power and can drive significant changes. In both instances, the power to effect the change came about through words. Consider your words as a way to bring light into your void emotional connection with your partner. If your relationship is a dying heart, consider your words as effective as CPR.

Theoretically, words hold as much power to connect with someone emotionally as they have to disconnect from them. Some people fall out of love with their partner simply because they stopped feeling the same affection they used to feel when they were still very new to the relationship. Whether spoken or written, how we use words can make others draw close to us or keep their distance from us.

The Positive Impact of Words

When used right, your words will easily support the growth of your relationship. It is like the law of attraction in Philosophy, wherein positive thoughts bring positive results into one's life while negative thoughts bring negative effects. In this instance, positive words in your relationship can positively impact your overall emotional connection.

Below are some of these positive impacts:

1. Trust building

Trust should be one of the foundational elements in any relationship. You and your partner need to practice open and honest communication so you feel comfortable trusting each other with anything. One way you can build trust with your partner is through language intimacy.

2. Conflict resolution

No relationship is without flaws; in every relationship, partners are bound to have issues. What is important is being conscious and intentional enough to ensure these issues never arise again. You can do that by speaking with your partner and ensuring they don't feel like they carry all the blame. This is the part where you discuss those issues calmly with them and find solutions that respect both your needs.

3. Mutual respect

Positive language outreach, such as appreciation and acknowledgment, is an excellent way to earn your partner's respect. But remember that respect is reciprocal. When your partner sees that you respect them, they, too, will respect you.

The Negative Impacts of Words

Do you still remember the Law of Attraction? How negative thoughts attract negative outcomes. This section will explore how miscommunication or negative words can negatively impact your relationship. These impacts usually come as one or more of the following:

1. **Misunderstandings**

One of the biggest pitfalls in communication is being misunderstood, which is especially true in relationships. Using vague, negative words can often lead to miscommunication, especially when you yell the words. If left unresolved, miscommunication can quickly breed misunderstandings.

2. **Self-esteem override**

Sometimes, we comment on or even criticize our partners for their input on some things, which only damages their self-esteem. Imagine calling a suggestion your partner made stupid. Even if their idea isn't feasible, there are better ways to express it.

3. **Barrier creation**

When you constantly push your partner away with your words, they surround themselves with a barrier where you can no longer reach them. You might notice your partner doesn't want to talk to you at this point because they are confident you will only mock their perspectives.

Now, you understand how powerful words are and how just one word can alter the direction of your relationship, either positively or negatively. That said, knowing what words to use and how to use them is key to connecting with your partner emotionally.

The Importance of Choosing Your Words Wisely

Think about a game of Scrabble. Each player has seven letters in their tiles, which they must arrange on the board to form different whole words. Your chances of winning the game depend on how critically you can think when it comes down to choosing the letters on your tile wisely enough to make a winning word.

This means that even if you are provided with all twenty-six letters in the English alphabet, you won't win if you don't know how to choose and use your letters correctly.

The same thing goes for your relationship. You will keep having issues until you become conscious and intentional about which words to use with your partner. Most people talk without ever thinking about the consequences. No word flies out of your mouth without an impact unless no one is on the receiving end,.

There is always a mental reception from your listener. It is safe to conclude that most people don't ponder the effect of their words because they are ignorant of the power of words. So, since you are here, how about taking a crash course to avoid this mistake?

Communication 101

In any relationship, communication exists as a bridge. Through this bridge, people can reach their partners, share their experiences, express their needs, and build a deeper understanding and connection.

However, just as a bridge can lead you to different stops depending on where you want to go, communication can lead to different situations influenced by your communication style. Simply put, using the wrong communication style with your partner will negatively affect them. You have to tailor your style based on their emotional needs.

When you adapt to your partner's preferred communication style, your day-to-day conversations will naturally improve, making it easy to avoid conflicts since there is mutual understanding. Even Marley Howard, LMFT —a marriage and family therapist — argued that disputes could be resolved faster if you understand your partner's tendencies while also being able to empathize with them to strengthen your relationship. In essence, do you know your communication style?

Communication Styles

The progression to communication is linear. Who we are tends to shape how we communicate with others; how we communicate with others tends to shape how we are viewed, and how we are viewed tends to define how people respond to us both physically and psychologically. In the same way, no two people are the same; everyone also has a distinct communication style, and knowing these styles can help you communicate better.

There are four significant steps of communication styles. Dr. Daria S. LaFave, a communication instructor at Southern New Hampshire University (SNHU), refers to these styles as instruments to help you understand others and learn how to relate better. According to her and other communication researchers, below are the four main styles of communication:

Passive Communication

Passive communicators barely do anything with words. Gilza Fort-Martinez, a Miami-based licensed marriage and family therapist, once called them "wallflowers." They prefer to accommodate anything when expressing their needs to avoid conflicts. They cannot say "No"; instead, they accept whatever their partner has in store for them.

However, their lack of expression results in their needs still needing to be met. This communication style is characterized by the willingness to submit to your partner's needs at the expense of invalidating your thoughts or feelings. As a result, passive communicators are more inclined to feel isolated in a relationship since their needs are not met due to their lack of communication.

Since passive people are more inclined to bottle up their feelings and not take charge, it weighs everything down on the partner as the entire relationship rests on them. Also, communication is a two-way process. Communication is hindered when only one person always takes charge in a relationship. It becomes problematic when you leave everything to your partner to decide because even they know they can be wrong sometimes. It is even worse when both people in a relationship are passive communicators.

Aggressive Communication

These communicators are often found dominating every conversation. Fort-Martínez labeled them as "the steamroller." They are the kinds of people who express their opinions or feelings in a way that invalidates and ignores other people's needs — they can technically be termed selfish communicators. Anger and judgment often drive their words, creating a hostile conversational environment with their partners.

They also quickly get defensive when their partners confront their opinions or feelings. As a result, aggressive communicators are more inclined to feel supreme in a relationship since their needs are almost always met.

Since aggressive communicators are the kind to override other people's emotions and dominate conversations, the consequence is that they don't listen to their partners at all. And we have established the fact that listening is essential in a relationship. You are more likely to get misunderstood when you are too ready to speak than listen. Misunderstanding is the last thing you want to fuel between you and your partner.

Passive-Aggressive Communication

These communicators usually stay on the fence — "the confuser," as Fort Martinez labeled them. They are hybrids, possessing the qualities of both an aggressive communicator and a passive communicator. In their two-faced nature, they may not outrightly communicate their feelings or needs but do so more indirectly by giving silent treatments or employing sarcastic responses.

Since their true intentions are always hidden, it's hard to know what they want, which may lead to confusion in a relationship. In essence, even though passive-aggressive communicators don't directly communicate their feelings, they still hold onto their negative emotions and let those affect their actions toward their partner.

Judging by how passive-aggressive communicators cannot voice their opinions, they quickly get irritated and frustrated. They are still angry even if they act indifferent to their partner's actions. They may say nothing is wrong and yet give you the silent treatment. When that happens, you might find yourself growing distant from your partner.

Assertive Communication

Communication experts see this as the ideal style of communication in a relationship. This is because, unlike the rest, an assertive communicator hinges on respect and clarity when expressing their needs. They do this without shoving their opinions down their partner's throats. They are the kinds of communicators Fort-Martínez labeled as "the self-confident."

The assertive style fosters open communication and mutual respect, leading to a healthier relationship. As a result, partners with this style tend to feel more safe and comfortable engaging in conversations. This is because they share their thoughts respectfully without imposing them on others. Assertive communicators recognize the differences between their partners and them, and this helps them build trust in their relationships. It is the style you want to adopt, as the other three are less effective in creating a healthy relationship. The following section sheds more light on how to go about this.

Adapting to the Right Communication Style

Before choosing the right communication style to interact with your partner, first figure out your default style. Knowing how you use words helps you determine your role during a conversation.

Once you have identified that your communication style falls within the other three styles, you must be intentional about moving toward the assertive style. This starts with knowing that while you have little power to change how your partner speaks, you can at least influence it. With the right communication style — the assertive, in this case — you won't have issues adapting to your partner's needs.

Here are a few steps to adapting to the correct communication style:

1. **Pause before responding**

It doesn't matter what kind of communication style your partner has; engaging with them more assertively by listening to them before you respond eases whatever tension can easily brew between your conversations.

2. **Model the conversation**

When your partner is an aggressive communicator, you can regulate the progression of the conversation by flipping both talking and listening simultaneously. This way, you create a safe space for them to voice their needs and make them understand yours.

3. **Let your actions match your words**

Keeping things from your partner is generally not recommended, especially concerning your feelings and emotions. So, when angry, don't suppress your feelings by always following your partner's preferences without expressing your own.

4. **Engage in face-to-face conversations**

Words impact us deeply and reduce miscommunication even more when spoken in person. You create a safe space between you and your partner when you talk to them face-to-face more often.

5. **Consult with a professional**

If, even after communicating assertively, an issue persists between you and your partner, do not risk the health of your relationship by hesitating to visit a professional.

By now, you have picked up how essential words are to building a healthy relationship between partners. Sometimes, you and your partner are distant because you no longer love each other but aren't expressing your love the right way or with the right words. With that in mind, let's dive into the language of love and how you can speak it.

A Look into Love Languages and the Psychology Behind Them

Before John married, he had promised himself that his wife would never do anything or get stressed out. So when John finally married Amy, he thought the best way to express his love was by doing things for her. As a result, Amy only did a few things. Before she woke up, John was done cleaning the house and doing the dishes; he also handled fixing the car and ensured their bills were paid on time.

One day, Amy could no longer stomach it again and cried. When he asked her what was wrong, she told him she really craved spending some time with him. Her love language was quality time with her partner, not acts of service. When John realized that even though his actions were much appreciated, they did not matter to his wife, who only wanted him to be present, he started scheduling regular date nights with her, and their bond deepened afterward.

Ever since Gary Chapman, Ph.D., published *The 5 Love Languages in 1992,* the concept of love language has been canonized, gaining a stronghold in the cultural lexicon as we know it today. Before he wrote the book, Chapman had noticed patterns in the couples he counseled. He saw how they misunderstood each other's needs, which led him to bring up the concept of a love language. Chapman suggested that everyone has their preferred way of expressing or receiving love.

In the story, John and Amy have different ideas about showing love. When John assumed that acts of service would be the best way to connect affectionately with Amy without asking her, he shot himself in the leg.

You shouldn't assume your partner's preferences. If your partner is a passive communicator, the consequence of unfiltered assumptions is that it slowly creates distance between you two. This is why you must know your love language and your partner's. Review your or your partner's attitudinal responses to properly assess the five love languages discussed below.

Words of Affirmation

Partners whose love language is words of affirmation treasure verbal communication of love more than anything else. All you need to reassure them of your love is to remind them how much you love them often and shower them with compliments, words of appreciation, and verbal encouragement. You can also stay connected by sending them encouraging texts or engaging with them on social media.

Couples' psychotherapist, Fariha Mahmud-Syed, MFT, CFLE, suggests that words of affirmation make your partner feel understood and respected. So, when words of affirmation are someone's love language, you could easily make their whole day just by complimenting them or telling them how well they are doing.

Dr. Michelle Rosser-Majors, an Associate Professor of Psychology, added that humans strive to feel capable, valued, and recognized. Positive words have this effect, laying the groundwork for strong, productive relationships with open, effective communication. Sometimes, consistent conflicts between you and your partner might not necessarily be because you did something terrible. It might be because you aren't acknowledging them with words.

Quality Time

Someone who sees quality time as their love language, just like Amy, wants you to be there with them. They value your entire presence with them compared to anything else. They are so emotionally connected to you that a little distance makes them feel like they are losing you. They tend to feel most loved when you shower them with undivided attention. This could be as simple as putting down your phone while talking to them to show their importance to you, making eye contact, and actively listening to them.

Mahmud-Syed described this love language as one that focuses on giving your undivided attention to a special person without indulging in distractions like television, phone screens, or other external interruptions. People with this love language deeply value spending quality time with their partner, engaging in meaningful conversations, or sharing recreational activities.

Dr. Chapman also agrees that quality time means giving someone your undivided attention and not sitting on the couch and watching television together. She recommended sitting on the couch with the TV turned off, looking at each other, and talking. The psychology behind doing this is that it emphasizes quality of time over quantity. Sometimes, all your partner demands from you is to be with them.

Acts of Service

When someone's love language is an act of service, they tend to value it more when their partner goes all out of their way to make things easy for them. This is where those partners who enjoy such acts as being fed breakfast in bed, being helped with pressing tasks when they've had a busy day, or being assisted with errands all fall into. Acts of service are simply lovely things you do for your partner to make them feel loved.

Mahmud-Syed claims this love language resonates with those who believe actions speak louder than words. Rather than hearing expressions of care, these individuals prefer to see appreciation through actions. They deeply value it when you take on small and large tasks to make their lives easier or more comfortable.

The psychology behind acts of service is that they create a warm, fuzzy feeling that your partner can connect to. Selflessness with your actions toward your partner inspires them to stand with you and connect with you no matter what.

Gifts

Gifts, as a love language, are pretty easy to understand and relate to. It is the act of being shown affection through "visual symbols of love," as Chapman says in his book. However, there is an underlying caution when gifts are your partner's love language. You must understand that it is not about the gift's monetary value but the thought behind it. People with this style tend to read meanings into how deliberately you pick gifts for them and what they represent in the relationship.

Mahmud-Sayed says that those whose love language is receiving gifts appreciate tangible and meaningful presents. The focus should be on giving items that hold significance for them and align with their values rather than your own.

Dr. Jeral Kirwan, former Program Chair of the Master of Arts in Psychology in the College of Health, Human Services, and Science at the University of Arizona Global Campus, provides valuable insight into the love language of giving gifts. He opines that there are psychological advantages to both giving and receiving. Giving a gift increases satisfaction and helps reinforce relationships by positively acknowledging each other.

Physical Touch

Partners who fall under this category appreciate physical contact with their partners. They feel loved when met with physical signs of affection, such as kissing, holding hands, cuddling, and sex. They are the ones for whom physical touch is the ultimate emotional connection. To them, it serves as an emotional connector. Usually, this is because they lacked physical intimacy in their childhood, so they seek it with their partners instead.

Mahmud-Syed comments that people who express appreciation through this love language feel valued through hugs, kisses, or cuddles when comfortable. They cherish the warmth and comfort that physical touch brings.

The psychology behind this love language goes beyond the surface level of thinking. It is just a touch. As infants, touch was the first language we spoke, and it is already imbibed in our behavioral patterns even as adults. In the *Scientific American,* Katherine Harmon, a researcher, stated, "Many children who have not had ample physical and emotional attention are at higher risk for behavioral, emotional, and social problems as they grow."

As a result, physical touch is quite integral in strengthening romantic relationships. For instance, imagine being in a conflict with your partner and resorting to hugging, cuddling, or kissing them on the lips; unless it is a grave issue, the conflict should be quickly resolved.

However, it is not enough to understand that these different types of love languages exist. You have to know which one works for you and your partner. Remember that it is a relationship. Your partner matters as much as you do, which means that while you need to learn about their love language, you must figure out what works for you and how it can strengthen your love.

How to Use Love Languages to Strengthen Your Relationship

The best things follow a particular pattern or systemic flow. Using love language follows the same metric. There is a system to it, but do not worry; by the end of this section, you should be adequately clear about how to tailor love languages to suit your relationship.

First, you should understand that you can only sew a cloth that fits perfectly with the proper measurements. It might fit, yes, but the goal is to fit perfectly. You have to find the right love language that fits your partner. Sometimes, even your partner might need clarification about their love language, so the weight rests on you. But not to worry; figuring it out is quite easy.

You could start by taking an online love language test on Gary Chapman's website to determine your and your partner's love language. You could also assess your past and present interactions with your partner, whether romantic, platonic, or even familial, and ask yourself when they feel most loved and most connected to you after using a specific love language. The same step goes for you. Try practicing each love language with your partner to explore how you feel about them, rating them from 0 to 100. Once you have identified your love language, you can move on with the lists of instructions below for each.

Words of Affirmation as a Love Language

If your partner's love language is words of affirmation, you can try using these positive and loving words:

- I love being with you.
- I love you.
- I love how much you help me.
- Your smile brightens my day.
- Your determination at work is so remarkable.
- I'm sure you will complete that task.
- I see how hard you are working on that task.
- You are such a compassionate partner.
- Your care and concern for our children gladden my heart.
- You look as gorgeous as always.

Physical Touch as a Love Language

If your partner's love language is physical touch, you could speak their language by doing the following:

- Cuddling
- Spooning
- Kissing
- Caressing
- Engaging in consensual sexual touch
- Snuggling
- Massaging

- Dancing
- Holding hands
- Placing an arm around their shoulder

Acts of Service as a Love Language

If your partner's love language is acts of service, here are lists of ways it can be spoken:

- Helping out with household chores
- Running errands
- Taking care of the children
- Mowing, raking, or gardening
- Walking the dog
- Doing the laundry
- Planning a trip or outing
- Putting gas in the car
- Making calls to the bank or the children's school
- Handling home maintenance
- Doing anything else that your partner doesn't feel up to doing

Giving Gifts as a Love Language

If your partner's love language is receiving gifts, here are things you can do to meet their needs:

- Find out what they like or make an educated guess.
- Consider your budget and buy them something nice without breaking the bank.
- Save in advance if it is expensive.
- Remember that the thoughts behind the gifts count more than the gift itself.

Quality Time as a Love Language

If your partner's love language is quality time, below are a few things you should try:

- Going on a trip or a vacation with them

- Putting down your phone while you are talking to them
- Going on a walk together
- Engaging in hobbies
- Trying out a new restaurant
- Spending a romantic evening together
- Having game nights
- Watching episodes of their favorite series with them

We've explored ways to strengthen your relationship with your partner using love languages, but know that love languages aren't a silver bullet to relationship issues. Sometimes, your partner might need more than a specific love language if their emotional nature demands it. For instance, your partner's love language might be hybrid, such that they are the type to prefer both quality time and gift-giving. Also, do not assume that all it takes to foster a peaceful and healthy relationship is understanding love languages. You need to be wary of and pay attention to more complex things.

Common Communication Pitfalls to Avoid

In every relationship, some traffic lights give order to smooth communication. But unlike the traditional traffic lights, there are only two signal lights herein: the red light, which signals "stop," and the green light, which signals "go." The red light encompasses those words you should stop saying due to how quickly they can escalate a conflict, while the green light includes those words you should learn to speak due to how healthy they can make your relationship.

What Not to Say and What to Say Instead

Unless you want to keep having issues in your relationship, there are certain things that you need to restrain yourself from saying because of their mental effects on your partner. Some of these statements include:

1. "You" statements

First, you must understand that arguments are a crucial part of communication for couples. Something is wrong in that relationship when everything is as smooth as day. However, you can learn how to effectively manage conflicts between you and your partner by avoiding the "you" statements. It is the kind of statement wherein you push all the blame on your partner by saying things like, "You don't listen to me," "You should have known better," or any other selfish "you" statement you can think about. Instead, practice using "I" statements. You could say something like, "I don't feel heard," or "I think we could do it this way too."

2. Threatening divorce

Some couples tend to blurt things without considering the consequences. One of them is the D-word. When you bring up divorce in the middle of a conflict, the mental message you are passing across to your partner is, "I'll leave if you don't a-b-c." Avoid that. You would only create a situation where your partner has to submit to you due to the threat, thereby creating a false trust between you. What you should learn to say instead is, "We have a problem, but how can we solve it?"

3. Saying nothing is wrong when something is

People who lie to themselves are more likely to find it hard to maintain a healthy relationship. This is why self-awareness is essential (as discussed in Chapter 1). Keep an open relationship. When something is wrong in your relationship, don't assume that your partner can read your mind or tell them that there is nothing wrong when there is. Tell your partner something is wrong and find a way to eliminate the problem.

More on Language That Provokes Escalation

By now, you should have picked up on how your words might have caused conflicts between you and your partner. You may have probably fallen into the communication pit of using "you" statements to blame your partner or the other pitfalls. Or maybe you used one of the following words that usually escalate conflicts:

1. No

This is not to tell you to never use the word "no"; it is simply to ask you to be very sensitive when using it. Do not just fling it all over the place. Usually, some people tend to tell their partners "no" to certain things even before they have fully understood what is being asked of them, and the mental response of their partner to that is hardly ever positive. In essence, don't be so quick to say "no." Ask clarifying questions first, and once you have thoroughly assessed the message and are entirely sure about it, you can go ahead and say it.

2. But

Whenever this conjunction is used in the middle of a sentence, it is to draw in negative addendums. For instance, imagine being in a conversation with your partner, and you said something like, "I understand you, but. . . ." It doesn't matter what comes after the word; you have already covered yourself with some defensive mechanism. Rather than saying that, you could use the coordinating conjunction "and" instead. So, you can say something like, "I understand you, and. . . "

3. Always

Generally, be wary of being too absolute in a conversation. Try to hedge as much as possible. The word "always" signals absolution and a finality you should try to avoid. When you ask your partner to "always dress the kids up," you aren't giving them a say in the matter or giving room for their opinion. So, remember to use the word sparingly rather than out of habit.

In this section, you've learned that your partner reacts to your words emotionally — positively or negatively, depending on the words themselves. This shows the ability of words to determine emotions. Thus, just as you can create a distance between you and your partner with the wrong words, you can foster an attachment to them if you use your words well. So, let's explore how you can get even more intimate with your partner through your intentional use of words?

Emotional Intimacy through Communication

What happens to a volcano wherein molten rock is rapidly trapped with pressure building? It would sooner or later explode. The same is true for humans. When you bottle up your emotions deep within you without letting your partner in, the result is an explosion. And trust me, nobody likes an outburst. You will only scare your partner away or even annoy them instead.

Understandably, some societal constructs almost bind us from discussing our emotions with people out of fear of being seen as vulnerable. For men, the stereotype is even a bit higher, as they don't want to be seen as weak, fragile, or whatever adjective the societal construct assigns to a man who talks about his feelings. But still, do it anyway. It will do you a lot of good. Expressing your feelings builds emotional intimacy between you and your partner, but how can you go about it?

Accept Your Feelings

Accepting your feelings means allowing them to exist without judging or invalidating them or even denying their existence. When you reject or stifle your emotions, you will most likely only make things worse, and this can ultimately lead to conflict and tension that can harm the emotional intimacy between you and your partner.

Describe Your Feelings

It is one thing to know that you feel somehow and another to identify those feelings. Try describing your feelings by writing them out or saying them out loud. Afterward, think about how to get them through to your partner so they can understand what is wrong with you. If you have difficulty naming your feelings, remember that most feelings usually fall under the following umbrellas: anger, fear, embarrassment, sadness, attack, hurt, and happiness.

Practice

Once you are done accepting and describing your feelings, the next step is to practice your expression with your partner. Try it by sitting them down and asking them to discuss their emotions. This will help ease you into talking about your own, too. Remember that slow and steady wins the race; starting small is fine.

We have discussed assessing your feelings, but what happens if it is the other way around? What do you do when your partner expresses their emotions to you? How do you validate them?

Validating Your Partner's Emotions

Have you ever seen your partner wear a brighter smile when you do something as simple as saying, "Thank you" for everything they do? Would you compare that bright smile to their reaction whenever they help you with something, and you don't acknowledge them because you think it is their job anyway? Can you see the picture now? That is exactly how validation can quickly turn a frown into a smile. It simply communicates to your partner how important they are to you.

The Importance of Validation

Compare these two scenarios: one, you just returned from work after such a stressful time or experienced a very stressful situation. When you finally got home, your partner confronted you, asking why you didn't do a particular house chore or still hadn't paid the utility bill. In the second scenario, you also had a long day at work. But when you get home, your partner comforts you and asks if you would love them to prepare a warm bath for you. In which of the scenarios do you feel more supported by your partner? The latter, yes.

Many people don't know how to validate their partners, and this is because they don't know how to identify or understand the feelings of their other half. However, when someone doesn't get emotional validation at tough times (and who says validation is for only tough times?), they may feel rejected, ignored, or judged by their partner. So, to connect strongly with your partner emotionally, you need to validate their feelings.

What to Say

There are many ways to validate your partner, but we only have a few pages to cover them, so we'll keep it simple. Ultimately, the trick to validation is pretty straightforward. As long as you show the other person that you recognize and accommodate their emotions, you validate them. So, you could say things like the following:

- I'm so happy for you! You deserve every bit of it. You've worked incredibly hard for this.
- Aw, that is so sad. I hope you will be fine.
- That was a huge accomplishment! We should celebrate it.
- Your boss said that? I would have been furious, too.
- That must have been so tiring for you.

What Not to Say

You invalidate your partner's emotions when you don't recognize or accommodate them. So, to prevent this from happening, avoid statements such as the following:

- It could have been worse.
- It is not that big of a deal.
- Stop crying over little things.
- Just put a smile on your face and wait it out.
- You'll be fine eventually.

Helpful Tips

To determine whether you are validating your partner enough, turn up the heat by following these tips. That way, you can connect intimately with your partner:

1. **Listen:** Active listening is non-negotiable. Avoid drowning yourself in your thoughts and losing out on what your partner is trying to share.

2. **Maintain eye contact:** Maintaining eye contact with your partner sends them a mental signal that they are all that matters to you at that moment, which is why you're focusing on them. This builds a safe space for them to connect to you.
3. **Time:** Expressing one's emotions takes quite a lot of time. Show your partner that you have all the time to be there with them through the process. Don't pressure them into opening up. They will only withdraw into their shell if you put too much pressure on them.
4. **Validate their feelings:** After your partner expresses their feelings to you, refer to the section above and ensure you validate them. This will foster more understanding and positive solutions, making your relationship healthier.

Interactive Element

We have been able to foreground the concept of love languages as posited by Dr. Gary Chapman: quality time, acts of service, physical touch, gifts, and words of affirmation. But I understand if you still don't know your love language. I've added a worksheet by Dr. Chapman below to help you determine your love language.

Instruction: read each pair of statements and circle the one that best describes you.

1. A. I like to receive notes of affirmation from you.

   E. I like it when you hug me.

2. B. I like to spend one-on-one time with you.

   D. I feel loved when you give me practical help.

3. C. I like it when you give me gifts.

   B. I like taking long walks with you.

4. D. I feel loved when you do things to help me.

   E. I feel loved when you hug or touch me.

5. E. I feel loved when you hold me in your arms.

C. I feel loved when I receive a gift from you.

6. B. I like to go places with you.

E. I like to hold hands with you.

7. A. I feel loved when you acknowledge me.

C. Visible symbols of love (gifts) are significant to me.

8. E. I like to sit close to you.

A. I like it when you tell me that I am attractive.

9. B. I like to spend time with you.

C. I like to receive little gifts from you.

10. D. I know you love me when you help me.

A. Your words of acceptance are important to me.

11. B. I like it when we do things together.

A. I like the kind words you say to me.

12. E. I feel whole when we hug.

D. What you do affects me more than what you say.

13. A. I value your praise and try to avoid your criticism.

C. Several inexpensive gifts mean more to me than one large, expensive gift.

14. E. I feel closer to you when you touch me.

B. I feel close when we are talking or doing something together.

15. A. I would like you to compliment my achievements.

D. I know you love me when you do things for me that you don't enjoy doing.

16. E. I would like you to touch me when you walk by.

B. I like it when you listen to me sympathetically.

17. C. I really enjoy it when you surprise me with something I love.

D. I feel loved when you help me with my home projects.

18. A. I like it when you compliment my appearance.

B. I feel loved when you take the time to understand my feelings.

19. E. I feel secure when you touch me.

D. Your acts of service make me feel loved.

20. D. I appreciate the many things you do for me.

A. I like receiving gifts that you make.

21. B. I really enjoy the feeling I get when you give me your undivided attention.

A. I really enjoy the feeling I get when you do some act of service for me.

22. C. I feel loved when you celebrate my birthday with a gift.

A. I feel loved when you celebrate my birthday with meaningful words (written or spoken.)

23. D. I feel loved when you help me with my chores.

C. I know you think of me when you give me a gift.

24. C. I appreciate it when you remember special days with a gift.

A. I appreciate it when you listen patiently and don't interrupt me.

25. B. I enjoy extended trips with you.

D. I would like to know if you are concerned enough to help me with my daily tasks.

26. E. Kissing me unexpectedly makes me feel loved.

    C. Giving me a gift for no occasion makes me feel loved.

27. A. I like to be told that you appreciate me.

    B. I would like you to look at me when we are talking.

28. C. Your gifts are always special to me.

    E. I feel loved when you kiss me.

29. A. I feel loved when you tell me how much you appreciate me.

    D. I feel loved when you enthusiastically do a task I have requested.

30. E. I need you to hug me every day.

    A. I need your words of affirmation daily.

Count how many times you circled the options lettered **A** to **E**. If **A** has the highest number of circles, your love language is words of affirmation. If you circled **B** the most, your love language is quality time. **C** means you prefer receiving gifts, while **D** means your love language is acts of service. And if **E** is the highest, your love language is physical touch.

Love Language Swap

Identifying your love language is one step toward nurturing emotional intimacy with words between you and your partner. Since communication goes both ways, you must recognize your partner's love language. This will help you understand how to relate to them better.

So, the first step in engaging in this love language swap is to intentionally understand your partner's love language by observing their interests. Afterward, devote an entire week to monitoring and inspecting your partner's love language, making even more intentional efforts to resonate with their emotional needs. However, know that this is bi-directional. Your partner should follow these processes just like you.

Questions to Deepen Your Bond

Once you are confident about the intentionality to know more about your partner's love language, and you have used a week to study their responses to each of the five languages, you can then move toward wielding words to deepen your emotional connection even more by getting to know more about them than they would readily disclose. Ask them these twenty-five questions:

- Where is a place you've always wanted to travel to?
- What have you always wanted us to do together but we haven't?
- What ranks highest on your bucket list?
- Do you want kids? If so, what values do you want to see in them?
- How do you foresee us resolving our persistent problems?
- How do you measure a happy life?
- Is there something you want to achieve that you need my help with?
- What is your weirdest habit?
- What is your family dynamic like?
- What are your most significant expectations for the relationship?
- What's the best vacation you have ever taken?
- What is your favorite childhood memory?
- What are the top quality adventures you've had in your life?
- What are those things you still regret?
- What is the most challenging lesson life has taught you?
- What do you consider your biggest success?
- What's your favorite food or snacks?
- What was your first impression of me?
- How do you intend to deal with stress?
- How would you describe your last relationship?
- Have you ever had your heart broken?

- How often do you get yourself checked for STIs?
- Do you think you are trustworthy?
- What's your wildest sexual fantasy?
- What do you consider cheating?

In this chapter, we have discussed how emotional intimacy can be nurtured through words. We did this by foregrounding the concept of love languages and how to identify them, including the common communication pitfalls to avoid in your conversations with your partner. We also discussed why validation is so important, and I shared some steps to help you and your partner validate each other's feelings. However, even after all these, conflict might still arise between you two. Therefore, in the next chapter, we will expound on how to deal with these persisting conflicts correctly.

Chapter

FOUR

N: NAVIGATE CONFLICT THE RIGHT WAY

“

"The aim of argument, or of discussion, should not be victory, but progress."

— Joseph Joubert

In 1986, Dr. John Gottman of the Gottman Institute designed a "love lab" where the interaction and approach of couples toward conflict were observed. In the study, he divided couples into two groups: he called one group the masters of relationships and called the other the disasters. While those masters had the best approach toward solving the conflicts in their relationships, the disasters showed four harmful behaviors, which Gottman labeled the Four Horsemen of the Apocalypse. These include criticism, defensiveness, contempt, and stonewalling.

The Four Horsemen is a biblical allusion to figures who are harbingers of doom and who represent the end of the world. In this context, the Four Horsemen refer to four harmful behaviors that escalate conflicts and ruin relationships. As you read on, we will analyze each horseman in detail and look at ways to navigate each one.

The First Horseman: Criticism

Most couples address conflicts with what Dr. Gottman called "harsh start-ups." These couples are usually quick to point fingers at their partner when an issue arises. This is where you would hear something like, "You are so self-centered. You only care about yourself." Most times, this happens because it's easier to point out other people's flaws and mistakes than to assess what the relationship needs to stay healthy, especially during conflicts. The consequence, however, is that it comes across to your partner as attacking and blaming, which will only further fuel the furnace of the conflict.

Antidote to Criticism: Soft Start-Up

It takes a lot of conscious effort for anyone to handle criticism well. Often, when we point fingers at our partner, it's because we have an unmet need, and we feel it's *their* responsibility to meet. But most of the time, we need some clarification about this need. So, before you point your finger at your partner to criticize them next time, try to understand your unmet need and why it bothers you so much. Once you do that, express the need with a "soft start-up." For instance, you could start a conversation with your partner using "I" statements rather than "you" statements. This helps you avoid being too confrontational or criticizing to your partner.

The Second Horseman: Defensiveness

In many instances, the first horseman is usually the cause of the second horseman. It's normal to immediately become defensive when we feel attacked in any context, but even more so in conflicts. When you criticize your partner by pushing specific blame onto them, they would immediately want to counter it by redirecting it back to you. And this will never get anything resolved.

Antidote to Defensiveness: Accountability

It's hard to resolve any conflict at all when you are still boiling. As an intentional partner, learn how to take a break and request breaks amid an argument to assess whether you have met your partner's needs. Once you realize that you haven't validated their needs, which led to the conflict, do not become defensive by trying to push the blame back on them. Take responsibility instead. Don't say things like, "It is not my fault we are late. You took forever to get ready." Say, "I didn't manage my time well, which contributed to us being late. I'll plan better next time."

The Third Horseman: Contempt

When you feel contempt toward your partner, you talk to them from a place of superiority and don't care about their needs. Even in Gottman's research, he concluded that contempt was the greatest destroyer of relationships and predictor of divorce and separation out of the Four Horsemen. Herein, the tendency to treat your partner with disrespect, mockery, sarcasm, and despise comes in. While contempt may sound like criticism, it isn't. The difference is that while criticism attacks your partner's behavior, contempt involves assuming a position of superiority over them.

Antidote to Contempt: Love/Appreciation

The antidote to contempt is simply love — appreciation is simply an offshoot. When you build an emotional culture wherein you talk to your partner with love, you will see how excellent your partner is. This is because what you focus on will determine what you see. When you focus too much on their opposing sides, you will only keep seeing that part of them. But when you switch up to embracing their positive sides, you get to see more of their excellent qualities. Dr. Gottman says contempt can be tackled with a "gentle start-up." When in the middle of a conflict, learn to express what you feel and the needs surrounding the situation; it will help you better manage the conversation.

The Fourth Horseman: Stonewalling

When you are the type of partner that stonewalls, you would rather leave the conflict scene than talk it out with your other half. Some couples believe that avoiding conflicts is much better than arguing it out, but this is wrong. Couples who stonewall do that because they get flooded with emotions and are too upset to respond. They choose to say nothing to avoid getting their partners angry. But when you don't discuss the issue in your relationship, you only breed resentment between you and your partner. And this may ultimately lead to the end of your love.

Antidote to Stonewalling: Self-Soothing

The antidote to stonewalling is direct. Just soothe yourself and calm down. It takes a lot of practice, but learning to embrace psychological self-soothing will go a long way in helping you curb this habit. When you are back in a calm state, you can actively listen to what your partner has to say and work toward solving the conflict.

From all we've discussed, one thing is clear: even healthy relationships face conflicts, but not everyone can be categorized into the Four Horsemen of Apocalypse. Nonetheless, it's not enough to recognize whether a conflict is major or minor; navigating it properly is even more important.

Tackling Conflict

When we generally talk about conflict, we mean the disagreement that can ensue between two or more people. But when we narrow it down to the relationship axis, we mean a dispute between two partners due to differences in opinions, experience, taste, perspective, personality, or beliefs.

For a marriage to be healthy, conflicts must be managed to a T to avoid emotional disconnection. However, it is impossible to manage a conflict you know nothing about, so reflection is essential when tackling disputes.

Why Couples Fight

The main reason couples fight is differences in needs. For instance, we discussed love languages in the last chapter and have seen how the inability to speak your partner's love language can hurt your relationship. You can't offer your partner something different from what their nature demands and expect them to be all happy about it. Other significant differences other than love language may contribute to why couples fight.

Top Things Couples Fight About

1. Sex

Research shows that sex is one of the major frequent sources of conflict between couples. Usually, the challenge is that one partner has a sexual desire that the other partner is unwilling or reluctant to fulfill. Some couples even fight over the lack of excitement in their sexual life due to lack of foreplay or improper sexual positions.

2. Money

This is another primary source of conflict among couples. Conflicts have a considerable tendency to skyrocket when cash is running short or couples are running into debt. When that happens, they may quarrel over how to get out of the debt or who is responsible for it. Usually, this is because couples rarely meet to discuss money management strategies early on.

3. Children

Children can also be a source of conflict in relationships when it comes to how many a couple want, if they want any, and whether the responsibilities are divided fairly. In some relationships, a partner may want to have a kid, while the other may not entirely be ready for it. Even when the child finally comes, there may be a conflict of interest about who should stay up in the middle of the night to watch over them or stay home to raise the child.

Why Do We Fight So Much?

Conflicts exist in every single relationship. As humans, we are naturally bound to disagree with people in some instances due to glaring differences. However, when conflicts get too frequent, an underlying issue needs to be looked into and adequately resolved.

One of these reasons is connection. Human beings are wired to seek love and connection from other people. That's why societies exist in the first place: that intense need to relate with others. But when this connection is threatened or broken, a conflict arises. This is because when the brain sends out a signal that a connection is threatened, there is a tendency to seek to regain that connection through dysfunctional, hurtful ways. Thus, rather than telling your partner, "I think we are losing our connection," you would rather nit-pick about their attitude instead. Sometimes, you even get passive about it and shut down instead, restraining yourself from worsening it.

Another reason conflicts ensue between partners is because one might be a pursuer. This insinuates that between the two, there is someone who feels the need to do more to sustain deeper communication or deeper connection. When the other partner doesn't reciprocate that same excessive need, the feeling of emptiness and loneliness comes from craving more. This is why you would hear your partner say something like, "I feel lonelier in this relationship than when I was not in any."

By now, you will have seen how much vulnerability exists in every relationship that brings conflicts, no matter your reflection on the factor of the conflict. It probably gets you wondering whether a relationship can exist without conflicts. Well, let's see.

Is Conflict Inevitable?

Have you ever come across someone whose ideas, feelings, thoughts, opinions, and experiences aligned with yours, even to the minutest detail? Conflict with such a person can seem impossible at first, but it isn't. We are all modeled in different ways. If genetic traits don't influence the differences between our partner and us, they would most likely be affected by other sociological factors. This makes it easy to conclude that conflict is inevitable in every relationship.

Searching for ways to eliminate conflicts from your relationship is a waste of time. You don't deal with conflicts by trying to eliminate them; you deal with them by ensuring that only healthy conflicts ever arise in your relationships. Interestingly, conflicts are often one of the best ways to know what is not working between you and your partner.

Conflict Can Be a Good Thing

At first glance, you might have been shocked by this title, wondering how conflict, of all things, could benefit you and your partner. But it can. The truth is that there is no way to know how different you and your partner are until a conflict arises from that difference. For instance, if you enjoy public displays of affection, but your partner doesn't, until a conflict ensues between you two, you may not realize your partner is uncomfortable with being showered with affection publicly. And when you don't know this, how can you work toward bridging the difference? This is why we need to understand what constitutes a healthy or unhealthy conflict in a relationship.

Unhealthy Conflict

This is characterized by a competitive mindset wherein partners view themselves as opponents in conflict. It is marked by the "you vs me" paradigm. This type of conflict tends to create a blame culture wherein an environment is built to either focus on personal victory or capitalize on pushing blame, rather than looking for a way to resolve the issue.

One sign a conflict is unhealthy is when both partners get defensive by protecting themselves and proving they are right without trying to understand each other. Another sign includes personal attacks wherein a conversation becomes a ground for personalized banters. Similarly, unhealthy conflicts are characterized by negative emotions which give room for high levels of frustration, anger, or even resentment in the relationship,

Healthy Conflict

Unlike unhealthy conflict, characterized by a competitive mindset, a healthy conflict is more attuned toward an inclusive mindset. This is to say that rather than partners seeing themselves as opponents, they stand together to address the real issue. You know a conflict is healthy when rather than embracing the "you vs me" paradigm when a conflict arises, partners embrace the "you + me vs the issue" paradigm instead.

It's easy to recognize a healthy conflict because both partners focus on uncovering the issue. Without resorting to personal attacks, the discussion relies solely on finding a solution to the root problem. Active listening also plays a significant role in healthy conflicts. Partners listen to each other's differences and find a way to solve them. They also prioritize constructive feedback by directing their feedback at the problem rather than criticizing each other.

However, when in the middle of an argument, it can be hard to think clearly about whether you are being constructive or destructive with your actions and words. A thin line exists between the two, and it is important to explore them if you would like to manage conflicts between you and your partner effectively.

Constructive vs Destructive Arguments

The main difference between constructive and destructive arguments is the approach toward resolution. While constructive arguments are geared toward more adaptive and collaborative behaviors to effectively solve a problem and achieve mutually beneficial outcomes, destructive arguments are geared toward escalation and avoidance. Usually, this is due to a desire to win that particular argument or walk away because one partner believes going back and forth with the other isn't worth it.

Using constructive arguments during a conflict is a reasonable approach to recognizing the differences between you and your partner and finding solutions to addressing those differences. The result is that it helps you maintain a good relationship with your partner and develop empathy toward understanding their needs better.

The consequence of approaching an argument destructively is that it only worsens the situation, leading to other problems. When we push blame to each other, we easily get distracted with how to respond with another blame rather than focus on what practical solution to use. In essence, destructive arguments only lead to unresolved and escalated conflicts.

How to Have Constructive Arguments

So far, I've stressed the importance of constructive arguments in having healthy conflicts. But while you now understand what it entails, it takes a systematic process to go about it. Therefore, here is a list of things you can do to have constructive arguments:

- Learn to be mindful and take a pause.
- Focus on the issue rather than seeing your partner as the issue.
- Show empathy and offer validation.
- Work with your partner to reach a resolution.
- Watch how you express your feelings without feeling attacked.
- Work with your partner as a team; it's a relationship, after all.
- Give your partner time to talk and ensure they do the same.
- Ask questions from a curious perspective rather than looking for a way to blame.
- Respect your partner's boundaries and stick to yours.

Undoubtedly, this section has exposed you to how to effectively manage and deal with conflicts by analyzing both healthy and unhealthy conflicts. But sometimes, managing conflict goes beyond offering constructive arguments. It extends to such things as apologies and forgiveness, and the next section explores how essential these two qualities are in conflict management.

On Apologies and Forgiveness

The love between two partners can be compared to a work of pottery. Overtime, when exposed to harsh conditions through conflicts and misunderstandings, it cracks. However, with Kintsugi — the

Japanese art form of mending a broken pottery with gold — the pottery can become whole again. In this instance, apologies are the Kintsugi to broken love. A study by Michael E. McCullough, Ph.D., Stephen J. Sandage, M.S., and Everett L. Worthington examined whether the effect of apology on our tendency to forgive is because of our increased empathy toward an offender who apologized.

They discovered that people tend to find it easier to forgive an apologetic person because an apology increases their level of empathy, and empathy can quickly breed forgiveness. McCullough and his colleagues published this research in the *Journal of Personality and Social Psychology*, supporting the hypothesis. However, it's important to note that not all apologies lead to forgiveness; only the meaningful ones do.

How to Apologize Meaningfully

Have you ever offered an apology and wondered why your partner still won't sympathize with you? One possible reason is that you're doing it wrongly. This reminds me of a woman who consulted a psychologist for guidance on what to do about her partner. According to her, it never felt genuine whenever her husband offered an apology after a conflict. It always went along the lines of: "I'm sorry, but. . ."

The moment you follow an apology with a "but," it's no longer an apology but an attempt to invalidate your partner's anger. What steps can you then take to ensure you are apologizing to your partner correctly?

1. Take responsibility for what you are apologizing for

This sounds difficult because taking responsibility in a conflict means swallowing your pride. However, when you are wrong, learn to admit that you are wrong. You don't need to keep trying to prove yourself right.

2. Be specific about why you are sorry

Most couples tend to do this. You would hear something like, "I'm sorry. I didn't mean it". Be more specific, and tell your partner what exactly "it" is.

3. Explain why you committed the offense

It doesn't matter whether the reason is stupid or understandable. Let your partner know what exactly led you to commit the offense.

4. Be sincere

Make sure there is no agenda behind your apology other than to glue the broken pieces of your relationship.

5. Don't react during an apology

It's a conversation. No fixed rule says that because it is an apology, your partner wouldn't cut you off or interrupt you, but don't react. Be patient and respect their feelings instead.

Just as the process of apologizing the right way takes intentional effort, so does forgiving your partner. Even if your partner considers all of these things, but you don't know how to forgive genuinely, it would all be a waste. And it would be your fault, not theirs.

How to Forgive Genuinely

While I encourage partners to consider forgiveness after a genuine apology, we need to face the fact that learning how to forgive doesn't happen overnight. You need to practice it consistently, which requires patience and trust building from both partners. But it is worth the stress. This is because when you permit yourself to let things go rather than hold up to stuck-up feelings, you feel mentally and emotionally free. Having said that, how do you forgive your partner genuinely?

1. Have an open discussion about what happened

When someone breaches your trust, it feels like you have been swept off your feet by a storm, but that's when honest communication is most important. When you understand the full scope of what happened, reaching a decision will be much easier.

2. Frame the situation

Remember that you shouldn't adopt a "you vs. your partner" mindset when addressing a problem but a "you + your partner vs. the problem" mindset. If your partner offends you, try placing yourself in their shoes to see things from their perspective and work toward finding a solution.

3. Set new parameters

If your partner offends you, consider reviewing the boundaries of your relationship to let your partner know what works and doesn't work for you. After assessing your partner's actions based on whether it respects your boundaries, you should create conditions that help you achieve forgiveness, such as reminding them how your parameters will be sufficient to avoid conflicts in the future.

Forgiveness is a bold and effective step toward resolving conflict in a relationship, but it isn't the only way. You might have to take other intentional steps after forgiving your partner. These steps give you an insight into what and what not to do during and after an argument with your partner.

Conflict Resolution Strategies

At this point, you know conflict is inevitable in every relationship, including healthy ones. After all, no two people can share exactly the same values and opinions and always agree. However, the key is not to try to avoid conflict but to learn how to effectively resolve it healthily.

For instance, you can express your thoughts and feelings directly to your partner more often. Bottling in your grievances to avoid disagreement with your partner is understandable, but you also need to speak up. Both you and your partner need to learn to be comfortable with sharing what bothers you.

Also, never blame your partner during a conflict. The temptation to push the blame of a conflict on your partner might be so glaring and overwhelming, but restrain yourself from giving in to it. Nothing good comes out of pushing blame. It only worsens the problem because you need to keep an eye on what is more important: how to resolve the conflict.

And most important of all, communicate. You have come across this particular word many times in this book that it probably sounds niche, but that's just how important it is. No healthy relationship can exist without proper communication skills, including active listening, maintaining eye contact, and decoding non-verbal cues.

The next three sections are dedicated to helping you learn to communicate your feelings better during an argument. We'll explore each section in detail, starting with things you shouldn't say during an argument.

What Not to Say During an Argument

1. This is all your fault

I've overemphasized the consequences of pushing blame around in a relationship. Pointing an accusing finger never helps during an argument. If anything, it hinders communication between partners and creates distance between them.

2. You're so [insert negative trait]

Focusing on your partner's flaws and mistakes in an argument can be likened to shooting yourself in the foot. It only ends up derailing the conversation from addressing the real issue. Also, it will always come up as being disrespectful to your partner.

3. But what about when you...

Trying to justify something terrible you did by bringing back a similar offense your partner once committed is unwise. Doing so sends them a mental message that you are the type who never forgives and would rather retaliate.

4. If you don't do this, I'm leaving

One of the things you should never do during an argument is threaten your partner with divorce or even hint at it. It might look like an excellent way to get what you want, but they will see themselves as nothing but an option to you.

5. It is either me or...

These kinds of statements only set you up for a win-lose situation because your partner's response is to take flight or wait to fight. And you can never be too sure of what the option will be. Besides, since they don't address the real issue, why say it at all?

What to Say Instead

Here is a list of fifteen statements you can say in the middle of an argument with your partner to foster a healthy resolution:

1. How do you feel right now?
2. I hear what you're saying, and I'm sorry you feel that way.
3. Did I contribute to you feeling like that?
4. Let's take a few minutes break so we can both calm down.
5. I understand that's how you see it.
6. Can we work together to come up with a resolution?
7. What can I do to make you feel better?
8. I'm sorry that I hurt you.
9. Could you please hear me out?
10. I don't feel good about this.
11. Please help me understand what you are trying to say.
12. What would you like me to do?
13. Can we try it one more time and be more objective?
14. We were both wrong at some point.

15. It is okay.

We've covered a lot concerning how to resolve a conflict in the middle of an argument. First, I explained the difference between healthy and unhealthy conflicts, as well as a constructive and destructive argument, by explaining and providing practical steps to take to approach the conflict during the argument. But what happens after an argument? What do you do?

Things to Do After an Argument

1. First, cool off

One thing you should never do after an argument is pretend that nothing happened and expect things to go back to normal. Just take some time and blow off some steam, then go back to the argument, calmly looking for solutions.

2. Give a heartfelt apology

When you apologize from your heart, it will soften your partner's heart. So, be as sincere as you can be with your apology. Sometimes, even an "I'm sorry" can carry so much weight.

3. Take responsibility

If, after an argument, you realize that you reacted all through it rather than listening to your partner, take responsibility for being rash and dismissive.

4. Solve the problem

After a conflict with your partner, try your best to make sure the problem gets solved. When you don't solve the problem that came up during an argument, you are literally engaging in an unhealthy conflict, and you don't want that, do you?

How to Stop Arguing and Keep Fights on the Minimum

It is normal for fights and arguments to happen in a relationship. However, one way to show that you are very much devoted to your partner is when you find a way to stop the arguments from reoccurring and keep the fights at the barest minimum, too. You could do that by following these practical steps:

1. Recognize your patterns

When you take your time to assess the harmful patterns in your relationship that lead to the conflict — including reliving the past, avoiding confrontation, competing to be heard, or not being present — you'll have taken one step toward solving the problem. It is usually easier to solve a problem after identifying it.

2. Rephrase your intrusive thoughts

Understandably, your intrusive thoughts would always want to get in the way of reasoning when it comes to an argument, but you have to learn to put a leash on them. When you don't throw out accusations to your partner, it reduces the possibility of a conflict.

3. Watch your tone

It's possible to say something positive but in the wrong way. That's why you should always watch your tone and ensure it's as calm as possible so you don't appear aggressive to your partner.

4. Listen

Research says that listening makes up about 45% of the time we spend communicating, and it's so sad that most people aren't good listeners. If you want to have a fluid conversation with your partner where there are fewer arguments and healthy conflicts, be big on listening.

Putting so much effort into managing your conflicts enhances the emotional connection between you and your partner, creating a space where a peaceful relationship thrives and flourishes. In the end, a relationship is only as peaceful as the partners in it.

How to Turn Conflict into Connection

There are four significant ways in which people respond to threats. These responses often present themselves in the four f's: fight, flight, fawn, or freeze. When we refer to the fight response as a way of responding to conflicts, we are talking about how partners tend to get aggressive when a dispute arises. Partners react to conflicts by fleeing from the threat for the flight response. Also, the fawn response is characterized by getting too indebted to your partner for your past mistake, making you do things you don't want out of weakness and desperation. Lastly, the freeze response involves a complete shutdown to avoid the threat. However, in each option, the root of the conflict isn't addressed, and there is an emotional disconnection between the partners.

When turning conflicts into avenues for emotional connection, you must take responsibility for learning new ways of thinking and behaving. This might include you understanding that just resolving conflict for the moment alone isn't enough, as you will only force temporary solutions that may not serve your interests in the end; you have to work toward resolving conflicts to foster your connection with your partner. What, then, are the practical steps you can take to turn your conflict into an intimate connection?

- Step into your partner's shoes.
- Communicate openly.
- Listen deeply.
- Seek solutions together.
- Frame your words with kindness.

Interactive Element

We have extensively discussed how to navigate conflicts correctly by exploring how to tackle conflict, how conflict can sometimes be a good thing to happen to couples, the importance of apologies and forgiveness, and the strategies for conflict resolution. Now, it is time to see how well you can manage your conflict, and this section will guide you.

1. Between you and your partner, schedule a specific place, date, and time for a meeting in the week. Allow at least thirty minutes for the meeting.

Meeting Place: ______________________________

Date: ______________________

Time: ______________________

2. Select one important issue you would like to resolve. List the specific issue or problem for discussion below:

____

____

3. How do you each contribute to the problem? Without blaming each other, list the things you each do that have not helped to resolve the issue.

Person 1:

1) ______________________________________

2) ______________________________________

Person 2:

1) ______________________________________

2) ______________________________________

4. List past attempts to resolve the issue that were not successful.

1) ______________________________________

2) ______________________________________

3) ______________________________________

5. Brainstorm better ways to resolve conflicts and choose the most effective that you and your partner can use. Do not judge or criticize any of the suggestions at this point.

1) ____

2) ____

3) ____

4) ____

5) ____

6. Discuss and evaluate each of these possible solutions. Be as objective as you can. Talk about how useful and appropriate each suggestion might be for resolving your issues.

7. After expressing your feelings, select one solution you both agree to try.

Trial Solution:

____

____

____

8. Agree on how you will each work toward this solution. Be as specific as possible.

Person 1:

____

____

Person 2:

____

____

9. Set a place, date, and time within the next week for another meeting to discuss your progress.

Meeting Place: ____

Date: ______________________________

Time: ______________________________

10. Pay attention to each other as the week passes. If you notice the other person positively contributing to the solution, praise their effort.

Mindfulness Practice Before Difficult Conversations

Once you have properly assessed and reviewed the worksheet above to know more about the problem between you and your partner and figured out practical ways to solve them, you need to practice mindfulness before your next difficult conversation with them.

Steps to Help You Prepare for a Difficult Conversation

1. Prepare the environment and make sure you won't get interrupted.
2. Take time to do a short guided meditation immediately before the conversation.
3. Stay mindful during the conversation — listen and pause before reacting.

In this chapter, we have unraveled the concept of conflict, the elements surrounding it, and how these elements affect the course of a relationship. I've also guided you through the process of engaging in productive conflicts that aid development and understanding. The next chapter will explore how arming yourself with proper emotional tools can help you achieve an even better relationship.

Chapter

FIVE

EQUIP YOURSELF WITH THE PROPER TOOLS

"

"Speak when you are angry and you will make the best speech you will ever regret."

— Ambrose Bierce

Whenever Maria was in the middle of a conflict with her husband Ben, she always got carried away by the heat of the moment and lashed out at him. After some time, she realized that her husband had grown increasingly distant from her after every dispute. She became scared that she was going to lose him because she couldn't control her emotions. Maria visited their marriage counselor for guidance, who advised her to always write down her feelings during a conflict instead of taking them out on her husband.

During another one of their heated arguments, Maria got angry, but instead of lashing out as usual, she decided to write down everything she wanted to say to her husband in a letter. After writing the letter, she tossed it aside until she was calmer the next day. With a clearer mind, she read the letter and realized half of what she wrote wasn't how she really felt. She became remorseful and approached Ben to calmly talk things out. They resolved the issue without Maria using the hurtful words she had written in the letter.

One thing is clear in this story: If Maria had continued lashing out her emotions at her husband, she might have lost him eventually, thanks to the growing distance between them. However, by writing down her feelings and not allowing them to get the best of her, she resolved the issue and patched things up with her partner. This shows that emotions can easily break a good relationship if not kept in check.

Why It's Best Not to Let Your Emotions Get the Best of You

When we're emotionally charged, we tend to be less logical and more emotional; in those situations, we may say or do things we usually wouldn't. At some point, we've all said or done something we wish we could take back. This is the same reason people are cautioned not to make promises when they are excited, or they may end up promising to do things they can't fulfill. It's also why it's inadvisable to talk when you are still very red with anger; you might end up saying hurtful things you can't ever take back. This is why emotional regulation is essential. You need to know how to put a leash on your emotions when they start influencing you. Simply put, ensuring you think before acting is crucial to emotional regulation.

Emotional regulation is the key to maintaining healthy relationships. It involves recognizing and managing your emotions effectively through measures that prevent them from ruining your good relationship with your partner. Self-regulating your emotional state will always stop you from doing or saying what might hurt the people you love and even yourself.

The essence of regulating your emotions in your relationship can't be overstated. Besides helping you avoid a mistake you might never be able to correct, it also helps you communicate more effectively with your partner, reducing conflicts and building trust and intimacy with them. On the other hand, the consequences of emotional dysregulation include misunderstandings and relationship breakdowns. This is why you need self-regulation in your relationship.

Below are some other importance of emotional regulation:

1. It promotes healthy communication

When your emotions don't blind you while you are angry or in the middle of a dispute, it allows you to have a clearer mind, giving you the room to communicate effectively with your partner without causing further disputes. Managing your emotions makes you less likely to react impulsively or say cruel things you don't mean, which will help you productively work through issues.

2. It helps you build strong emotional bonds

Another critical aspect of emotional regulation among partners is that it helps them build strong emotional bonds that strengthen their love ties. When you can restrain your emotions' control over you, you'll find it easier to empathize with your partner and understand their viewpoints during conversations with them. That way, you'll foster emotional intimacy between you two and strengthen your emotional bond.

3. It aids conflict resolution

This is one of the most important advantages of practicing emotional regulation. It helps you avoid unnecessary conflicts with your partner and build a healthy relationship with your partner instead. Sometimes, your partner's actions or words might provoke you and make you emotional, but regulating your emotions will help you approach things objectively instead of subjectively. When you can put your feelings aside during a heated situation and address it logically, you'll approach resolving conflicts calmly and rationally, yielding practical and effective solutions.

Now that you know just how important emotional regulation is, let's dive into how to achieve it in your relationship.

Processes Involved in Emotional Regulation

There are several ways to regulate your emotions, which we will look into. Since emotion is a delicate part of human psychology, learning to manage and keep them in check might require so much effort. But don't worry; we will look at some detailed step-by-step instructions to help you master emotional regulation seamlessly. Once you have mastered regulating emotions, bringing the knowledge into your relationship will help it flourish.

These instructions are cushioned into the various practical techniques and strategies for effective emotional regulation below. They include breathing exercises, mindfulness meditation, anger management techniques, self-soothing strategies, practicing patience, and mastering the art of non-reactivity.

Breathing Exercises

Have you ever wondered why meditation in yoga includes taking deep breaths? It is because one deep breath is enough to change the progression of your focus, mood, and even the rest of your day. It might seem unbelievable, but that's how powerful breathwork can be when you do it correctly. This is why it is a vital part of many therapy and fitness practices.

Breathwork involves being aware and in control of your breaths and using them to change your physical, mental and emotional state. The autonomic nervous system is responsible for the body's involuntary functions. For instance, when you are anxious, your hands may start shaking due to the influence of the autonomic nervous system. However, it has been discovered that there are ways to trick the system. For instance, just by speeding up your breath, you can become more alert and anxious; likewise, when you slow it down, you can key into the calmer and more focused part of you. However, doing this right takes practice.

Different Types of Breathwork

Each type of breathwork has some peculiar functions and benefits to them. In this section, we'll look at the different types of breathwork and the benefits of each one.

Diaphragmatic Breathing

This is also known as "belly breathing." The breathing technique involves you inhaling fully, thereby expanding the belly as much as you can, then compressing it so that the breath you have inhaled can be released. In this technique, as the diaphragm expands, your belly does the same. This breathing exercise is suitable for beginners, and it helps foster a mind-body connection.

Follow these instructions to practice diaphragmatic breathing:

- Sit or lie down with one hand on your stomach.
- Place the other hand at your side or on your chest.
- As you breathe in, notice your stomach expand with the inhalation.
- As you exhale, notice your belly contract and grow smaller.
- The hand on your belly should move more than the hand on your chest.

Holotropic Breathing

This breathing technique was developed and practiced as an alternative to mood-altering drugs because of its ability to lure you into an altered state of mind. It is achieved through even breathing patterns and movement repetitions and monitored by a facilitator. In the altered state — which many people consider to be a state of elevated consciousness — you can break through the trauma and emotional blocks that would have proven otherwise to surmount. Because the holotropic breathing technique requires the supervision of a facilitator, the methods won't be discussed here.

Breath-Focus Breathing

This is a simple breathing technique that uses imagery or focus words. In it, you choose a focus word that helps you feel relaxed and makes you smile or a word that is simply neutral. It can be any word as long as it enables you to focus and is something you can repeat every time through your practice.

Here's how to practice breath-focus breathing:

- Sit or lie down in a comfortable place.
- Bring your awareness to your breaths without changing your breathing pattern.
- Switch between normal and deep breaths occasionally. Note the differences between the normal breathing and the deep breathing.
- Notice how your abdomen expands by inhaling deeply.

- Note how shallow breathing feels compared to deep breathing.
- Practice deep breathing for a few minutes.
- Place one hand below your belly button and keep your belly relaxed.
- Notice how it rises with each inhalation and falls with each exhalation.
- Let out an audible sigh with each exhale.
- Start the practice of breath focus by combining this deep breathing with the focus word you have thought about, coupled with imagery to support your relaxation.
- Imagine the air you inhale bringing peace and calm throughout your body.
- Try saying "inhaling peace and calm" mentally.
- Imagine the air you exhale, flushing away anxiety.
- Try saying "exhaling tension and anxiety" mentally.

Humming-Bee Breathing

This breathing technique is especially noted for its ability to help create an instant calm and soothing feeling around your forehead with its unique sensation. Some people even tend to use the humming-bee breathing technique to help them relieve their frustration, anger, and anxiety. Research published by the National Library of Medicine in 2017 also claims it may help reduce your heart rate and make you feel less irritable and stressed.

Follow these steps to practice the humming-bee breathing:

- Choose a seating position that is comfortable for you.
- Close your eyes and relax your face.
- Place your two index fingers on the tragus cartilage (the part that serves as a partial cover for your ear canal).
- Inhale and gently press your fingers into the cartilage as you let out the breathing as an exhale.
- Do this while keeping your mouth closed; you should hear a loud humming sound.
- Continue doing this for as long as you are comfortable.

Mindfulness Meditation

Mindfulness meditation is a mental training practice that teaches you to slow down your racing thoughts, be free of negativity, and calm your mind and body. It is a practice that combines both meditation and the art of mindfulness. This mental state involves being entirely focused on the present so that you can acknowledge and accept your thoughts and feelings without judging them.

While the techniques for practicing mindfulness vary, they generally involve deep breathing and awareness of both the body and mind. Mindfulness also doesn't require any props at all. You don't need candles, essential oils, or even mantras. All you need to get started on mindfulness meditation is a comfortable place to sit, some free time, and a mindset void of judgment.

Guided Meditation

You need to understand that these techniques are as important to your partner as they are to you. Thus, if you notice that your partner is blinded by their emotions, you could bring them back through a guided meditation, taking them through the flow. They could do the same for you when *you* get blinded by your emotions.

In this section, we'll look at three short guided meditation scripts you can use with your partner to help them relax and regain their calm. Note that you have to speak slowly and softly for the best effect.

A Two-Minute Guided Meditation Script to Help Your Partner Find Calm

- I invite you to take a deep breath, and when you're comfortable, close your eyes [pause].
- Take a moment to imagine yourself being more calm, peaceful and focused [pause].
- As you allow your subconscious mind to create a picture of what calm looks like, consider what you might be seeing

[longer pause], hearing [longer pause] and what you might be feeling that shows you are more calm, peaceful and focused [pause].

- Perhaps, by now, you are already feeling more calm, peaceful and focused [pause].
- If not, key into your unconscious mind and see how it can reveal how you might do this [longer pause].
- Once you've done that, know that it can be this easy to create a little more calm in your life [pause].
- Again, I invite you now to take a breath for a moment and begin to return your attention back to the room, listening to the sounds around you and begin to open your eyes [pause].
- So, how was that?

It is said that this particular guided meditation script uses the Ericksonian Hypnosis and NLP techniques to allow the client to picture for themselves how calm looks or what it feels like and how to bring it into their lives.

A Three-Minute Guided Meditation Script Using Breathing

- I'd like you to pause, take a deep breath, and place your feet flat on the floor. Feel the ground underneath you with your feet.
- Place your hands on your stomach and take two to three deep breaths. Notice the rhythm of your stomach rising and falling with each inhalation and exhalation.
- And once you feel comfortable, you can close your eyes.
- As you keep breathing, inhaling deeply into your stomach, I would love for you to breathe in for a count of five. Hold it for another count of five, then exhale slowly for a count of five. Keep up with the rhythm, breathing in for five, holding it for five, and exhaling for five [longer pause].
- Great. I'd like you to slowly bring your attention back to the room. Notice the sounds around you and begin to open your eyes [pause].

- So, how do you feel now?

This guided meditation script can help revitalize and relax your partner when they're restless or furious. Deep breathing helps oxygenate their blood, while focusing on their breath helps calm their nerves and brings them back to the present.

A Five-Minute Guided Meditation Script for Relaxation and Body Tension Release

- I'd like you to get comfortable and relax. Take a deep breath and place your feet on the floor, feeling the surface of the ground underneath you. Then, take a few deep breaths for a moment [pause].
- I'd like you to start by focusing on your toes. Try scrunching them up, then release them [pause]. Relax your ankles [pause] — now, your calf muscles [pause]. Remember to let all your thoughts flow away in a bubble.
- Now relax your buttocks [pause] — your pelvic area [pause]. Then, begin to pay attention to any tension you may feel in your back [pause]. Now, your shoulders. Try lifting them and releasing them completely.
- Wonderful. You are doing well [pause]. Now, it is time to relax your neck and jaw muscles. Take a deep breath, then as you exhale, let go of any tension you hold in your neck and jaw [pause]. Finally, move to the top of your head [pause]. Hunch your shoulders up one last time, and as you release them, let any remaining tension flow out of you.
- Take a few more breaths and enjoy the feeling of relaxation for some time [longer pause].
- [softly] I'd like you to bring your attention back to the room slowly. Begin to notice the sounds around you, and when you are ready, open your eyes [pause].
- So, how do you feel now?

This guided meditation is known for its ability to help you focus on and purposefully relax your entire body, one part at a time.

Body Scan

Just as the name suggests, a body scan is a form of mindfulness meditation that involves focusing all your attention on your body, guiding the mind systematically on different body parts, and redirecting your focus to your body when you get distracted.

It is often used as part of a longer Mindfulness-Based Stress Reduction (MBSR), with benefits that include deep relaxation, lowered stress and anxiety, and improved sleep. It would be insufficient to talk about the importance and advantages of a body scan without outlining its process. Thus, here is a brief and helpful body scan script from Kabat-Zinn's bestseller *Wherever You Go, There You Are: Mindfulness Meditation in Everyday Life*:

- Focus on your breathing as you lie down.
- Sense your breath moving through your entire body.
- Bring your awareness to different areas, such as your feet, legs, pelvis, belly, chest, back, shoulders, arms, throat, neck, head, face, and the crown of your head.
- Listen closely, allowing yourself to feel whatever is present fully.
- Observe how the sensations in your body shift.
- Notice how your feelings about these sensations evolve.

Visualization/Guided Imagery

Guided imagery uses the power of imagination to stimulate all your five sensory channels, leveraging on inner self-talk while using affirmations. The effectiveness of this particular technique lies in the fact that the human brain and related neurophysiology find it almost impossible to distinguish between what is imagined and what is real sometimes. As such, we react to our imaginations almost in the same way we react to what is real. That said, there are three main practical techniques of visualization:

Guided Affective Imagery

This technique helps people who have trouble staying in touch with or expressing their feelings in relation to real-life events. Guided affective imagery works using a random mental image generated by you or your partner (depending on who the mediator is). First, you are required to lie down and do relaxation exercises. Then, the mediator suggests an imagery theme, such as walking up a mountain, hiking, or scaling a mountain, after which you are asked to describe that journey in terms of the random images that arise.

Scripted Guided Imagery

This particular technique begins with a relaxation technique, then the partner on the receiving end of the practice is led through an imaginary journey using a script. Usually, the script helps the partner solve a subconscious problem using effective symbolism and multi-sensory visualization.

Imagery and Drawing

This is a more familiar technique, with its roots in art therapy. In imagery and drawing visualization, you ask your partner or are asked by your partner to draw the image being described. This is very useful when you want to manage trauma because trauma can sometimes make it hard to talk, preventing you or your partner from voicing your frustration. However, that emotion can be expressed with shapes, colors or expressive images.

To engage in visualization activities, you can go through this simple exercise:

- Sit back, relax, and close your eyes. Picture a peaceful place, like a forest, a movie theater, a beach, or any spot that brings you calm.
- Visualize what you can see, hear, and smell in this tranquil place. Begin breathing slowly, allowing your lungs to fill with air. Hold your breath briefly.

- Slowly exhale while picturing your surroundings. Focus on what you can see, hear, and smell. With each breath, notice if there's any tension left in your body, and allow it to drain away.
- As you breathe in and out, release negative thoughts from your day. Free your mind of worries while you hold on to this comforting image.
- Absorb the serenity of the moment, letting the calmness of your peaceful place wash away stress and release any tension from your muscles.
- How do you feel now? Do you feel more relaxed?

Progressive Muscle Relaxation

This exercise helps you relax your mind and body. It involves tensing your muscles for about five seconds without straining them. Feel free to omit this step if you notice any difficulty with any of your muscles during this process. Also, it would help if you breathe during this practice. Let's use the adaptation from *The Anxiety and Phobia Workbook* by Edmund J. Bourne:

- Start by finding a comfortable sitting or lying position where you won't be disturbed.
- Focus your attention on your body, and if your mind starts to wander, gently bring it back to the muscle you're working on.
- Take a deep breath from your abdomen, hold it briefly, then exhale slowly. As you breathe, notice your stomach rising and your lungs filling with air.
- With each exhale, imagine any tension flowing out of your body. Breathe in, breathe out, and begin to feel yourself relaxing.
- Remember to keep breathing as you progress through each step.
- Raise your eyebrows to tighten the muscles in your forehead, holding them for about five seconds, then release all the tension.

- Pause for about ten seconds.
- Feel the weight of your relaxed head and neck sinking.
- Breathe in and out.
- Release any stress, then clench your fists firmly without straining. Hold for five seconds, then let go.
- Pause for about ten seconds.
- Flex your biceps, feeling the tension building. Visualize the muscle tightening. Hold for five seconds, then release and enjoy the feeling of relaxation.
- Breathe in and out as you tighten your triceps by extending your arms and locking your elbows. Hold for five seconds, then release.
- Pause for about ten seconds.
- Tense your upper back by pulling your shoulders back, trying to bring your shoulder blades together. Hold for five seconds, then release.
- Pause for about ten seconds.
- Tighten your chest by taking a deep breath and holding it for five seconds, then exhale.
- Tighten your abdominal muscles by pulling them in. Hold for five seconds, then release. Pause for ten seconds.
- Gently arch your lower back, holding for five seconds, then relax.
- Pause for about ten seconds.
- Feel your upper body letting go of stress and tension, holding for five seconds, then relaxing.
- Tighten your glutes, then imagine your hips relaxing.
- Tighten your thighs by pressing your knees together as if holding a small object. Hold for five seconds, then release.
- Flex your feet by pulling your toes toward you, feeling the tension in your calves. Hold for five seconds, then let your legs sink down in relaxation.
- Pause for about ten seconds.
- Curl your toes under to tense your feet, then release.
- Imagine a gentle wave of relaxation spreading from your head down to your toes.

- Feel the weight of your fully relaxed body.
- Breathe in. . . and out. . . in. . . and out.

Anger Management Techniques

Earlier, I mentioned that one major consequence of not regulating your emotions is that you might do something you would regret later. As with other emotions, if you don't manage your anger, it can lead to various problems in your relationship, including domestic violence. However, managing anger doesn't mean erasing it completely. It means learning to express it healthily and productively. Having said that, what are the strategies for anger management?

1. Identify your warning signs

Anger builds up in people differently. For some people, it happens instantly, while others might feel their anger build gradually. However, there are usually warning signs for each person based on their style. When you recognize them earlier, it gives you the leverage to manage them effectively.

2. Run from the triggering situation

By now, you might know certain discussions lead to unnecessary arguments with your partner and could make you angry. Rather than remain in such situations, why not avoid them so you can avoid getting triggered?

3. Talk through your feelings

For your relationship to be healthy, you must build a strong connection between you and your partner such that you both find it easy to open up regarding anything at all. This safe space can also help you manage your anger. By talking about how you feel, you not only get to ease the burden but also get someone willing to lend a helping hand.

More on Emotional Management Techniques

Remember the story of Maria, who saved her marriage by implementing an emotional management technique? I get that your relationship might be hanging on a thread like Maria's, which is why I'll share different techniques with which you can effectively manage your anger when it arises:

1. Count to twenty before saying anything.
2. Leave the room for several minutes or hours, if necessary, before discussing sensitive issues that may provoke your anger.
3. Write a response to a problem before tackling it orally or in an argument.
4. Keep a diary where you document your negative emotions so as to get them away from your system.
5. Consider getting a pet, as studies show that they sometimes help to reduce blood pressure levels and harmful substances in your system.
6. Talk about these provoking situations with a trusted friend and vent to a therapist.

Self-Soothing Strategies

Have you ever heard people say, "I listen to music because it calms me"? The truth is, there are several ways to calm your body when an external factor disturbs its peace and music is just one of them. But there are others, and they are termed "self-soothing strategies."

Self-soothing activities don't necessarily have a fixed process. They include anything that brings calm to your sympathetic nervous system. They bring this said calmness by activating your parasympathetic nervous system, which is the rest-and-digest state.

There are several self-soothing techniques to help you find calm through your anxiety, anger or other emotions:

1. Breathe deeply

I've said before that breathing has the power to alter the state of the mind, which is why it is essential in meditation. Closing your eyes for some time and breathing deeply can help you focus and maintain calm.

2. **Have a good cry**

As odd as this sounds, crying is quite effective for self-soothing. A 2020 study suggested that crying is a way to relieve stress and release your emotions. It tends to lower the stress hormone cortisol and regulate your heart rate instead.

3. **Listen to music**

You can curate a playlist of music that makes you feel better. Whenever you notice some disruption in your peace, you can return to the playlist and drown in it.

4. **Try out grounding techniques**

Activating your senses can help ground you in the present moment. Some ways you could do this include curling up with your favorite book or movie or even cuddling your pet.

More on Grounding Techniques

Grounding is a practice that helps disinfect you from unwanted flashbacks, memories and negative emotions that distract or weigh you down. This exercise offers the right assistance through which you can refocus on the present moment, distracting yourself from other unnecessary feelings.

There are two primary techniques to grounding: the physical grounding and the mental grounding. While physical grounding techniques focus on using the five senses or tangible objects that can be touched to manage your stress properly, mental grounding techniques use mental distractions to redirect you from stressful thoughts back to the present.

Practicing Patience

You will always find yourself in situations that test how much you can hold your cool. Even if you don't put yourself in those situations, rest assured that someone will put you in them. There is no escaping it. But do you fight over everything plunged at you when you can resolve the issues effectively? That is why practicing patience is an essential part of emotional regulation.

The Importance of Patience

Many dictionaries define patience as the ability to endure delays, problems, or suffering, but it goes beyond this view of acceptance or adaptability. Patience also involves maintaining utmost composure at the onset of challenges. Although practicing patience isn't something you learn in a day, its importance can't be understated. Here are some of them:

- **Peace**: When you hardly get bothered by an external factor, it brings peace of mind.
- **Clarity**: The truth is that being impatient will rob all your attention and focus, letting you channel them into a dispute instead. However, with patience, you regain that clarity.
- **Active listening:** By being patient with your partner, you have ample time to listen to their needs and assess them before you respond rashly. This helps you build an emotional bond with your other half.

Ways to Be More Patient with Your Partner

If there is one thing you should always have at the back of your mind before reacting to your partner's actions rashly, it's your marriage vows to stand with them at their best and their worst. But the only way to fulfill that promise is through patience. It's important to learn to be more patient with your partner, and you could do this effectively through the following tactics:

1. Bite your tongue

Sometimes, we can't detach from our pent-up anger because it is a part of us. But before you say anything during this period, try biting your tongue softly for a few minutes. This tends to keep you from speaking impulsively.

2. Ask again

Just as a fast-food worker repeats your order to avoid misunderstanding, you can be more patient with your partner by repeating what they said to be sure you heard them correctly. Conflicts often happen because of misunderstandings in communication.

Have it at the back of your mind that patience mainly rests on one element: non-reaction. The ability to pause before you react is what makes you patient. That's why you need to learn the art of non-reactivity and how to use it in your relationship effectively.

Mastering the Art of Non-Reactivity

Being non-reactive means learning to consider and evaluate what has been said or done before responding thoughtfully or realistically. Mastering the art of non-reactivity means fully understanding the concept of choice. In every situation, you have the choice of either reacting or doing the more productive thing, which is being unreactive. For example, you might catch your partner saying negative things about you with her friends. But rather than flare up immediately, you could try to assess how much truth is in what she said.

There's a process to learning how to be non-reactive in conflicts, and getting started is easy. All it takes is to follow the steps outlined below:

1. Speak more from curiosity, not a conclusion

If you'd like to be more intentional about your responses to your partner, you need to slow down and be more curious about what they say rather than quickly conclude what you think they have to say.

2. Get back into your body

Start by planting your feet on the floor, then uncrossing your arms. Relax your shoulders and belly, then slowly go down and down on your feet, crouching. This tends to reverse the domino effect of emotional triggers on your body. Once you are sure you have gotten back into your body, then you can respond.

3. Make the other person right

Rather than look for faults to criticize in what your partner says about you, you can be more effective by scanning through their words, picking those that are right about you, then working on them.

4. Don't take things so personally

When we take things too personally, we plunge into a state of an amygdala hijack. So, breathe instead. Reclaim the possession of your total consciousness, then shift your perspective from being too blinded by anger to being able to concentrate.

So far, we have discussed the importance of emotional regulation in a relationship and the extensive step-by-step processes and strategies to go about it. In the next chapter, we will explore how the intentional practice of emotional regulation and other techniques can help create closeness between you and your partner.

Chapter

SIX

CONSCIOUSLY CREATE CLOSENESS

> *"The best proof of love is trust."*
>
> **— Joyce Brothers**

Understanding Trust

The trust between two partners can make a relationship stand the test of time. When partners trust each other, there is no room for suspicions of infidelity when one partner is caught talking to someone or when they return home late. Naturally, a relationship strengthens when these doubts and insecurities have no place in it.

However, when there is no trust in a relationship, the two partners usually end up unhappy. This is because instead of channeling their energy into improving their relationship, they become too conscious of their partner's actions and spy on them. This is why partners need to prioritize building trust before anything else.

Trust can be described in many ways. However, at its core, it's being confident that your partner is always honest with you, no matter how hard it is, and that there is nothing hidden in your relationship that could hurt you.

7 Elements of Trust in a Relationship

Most times, some partners do intend to build trust in their relationships, but they don't know what components make up trust. Thus, when it comes to building trust in your relationship, your intention isn't enough. You have to learn the elements that constitute it, and they are listed below:

1. Boundaries

Setting boundaries in a relationship may seem unnecessary at first because you think you should accept everything your partner does and vice versa. However, it's healthier to set clear and honest boundaries in your relationship so you and your partner can express your needs with certain limits. When there is mutual respect for the boundaries set, you know you've built trust with your partner.

2. Reliability

This is the foundation of trust itself in any relationship. When you are always reliable, your partner feels more confident trusting you to get things done.

3. Accountability

Always learn how to take responsibility for your shortcomings and mistakes. When you always hold yourself accountable when wrong, you show your partner that you are willing to address mistakes in the relationship, which is a basis for building trust.

4. Vault

This refers to that safe place you create with your partner for saving confidential information about each other that you never share with other people, no matter what. When you practice discretion with your partner's secret, it enhances the trust they have for you.

5. Integrity

You demonstrate integrity by staying true to your beliefs and values no matter how challenging they become. When you consistently show your partner that you're honest, it builds trust in them to keep opening up to you.

6. Non-Judgment

This involves creating an open relationship where you and your partner get to talk and share sensitive things without fearing being judged. When you hinge on empathy rather than judgment, it increases the chances of your partner trusting you.

7. Generosity

This does not involve material things. It involves emotional generosity instead. When you always give your partner the benefit of the doubt in situations where their actions do not exactly meet up with your expectations, it builds up the idea that you trust them in their mind, and they will reciprocate with the same.

So far, we've talked at length about trust and its elements, but it's hard to appreciate a bit of knowledge whose importance you don't know. In the same way, you may not know what to do with your understanding of trust until you see how important it is in holding down the reins of your relationship.

Why Is Trust So Important in a Relationship?

Trust is a vital component of a happy and successful relationship. In fact, you can have all the qualities we discussed in the previous chapters but still have a shaky relationship if you don't have trust. Imagine showering your partner with gifts as a love language, but they don't even trust the motive behind the present. This and the following are reasons why trust matters a lot between partners:

1. It encourages forgiveness

When there is trust between you and your partner, there is a higher tendency to easily forgive each other for your shortcomings and undoings rather than battle it out. This is because you believe in them due to the trust that they have established over time.

2. It fosters intimacy

Establishing trust creates a strong bond and foundation between your partner and you. When you know you can trust your partner no matter what they do or where they are, you'll feel safe, and your intimacy will increase.

3. It reduces conflicts

Trust is the most effective way to navigate conflicts in a relationship. The rest are simply complementary. We are more likely to accommodate our partners and look for solutions when we trust them enough to know they're better than whatever a conflict tries to make you believe they are. Trust makes you give people the benefit of the doubt.

The Consequences of Lack of Trust

Trust is the glue that holds a relationship together. When it fades, the entire relationship falls apart. But this doesn't happen instantly; usually, it starts with the following consequences whose ripple effect leads to the relationship's breaking apart:

1. Constant suspicion and jealousy

One consequence of a lack of trust in a relationship is that it makes people suspicious and jealous of their partners. When that happens, you might start questioning your partner's every move and even scrutinizing their interactions with other people. As a result, you and your partner would feel like you're walking on eggshells and struggle to feel comfortable around each other.

2. Frequent arguments and misunderstandings

A lack of trust also breeds frequent arguments due to misunderstandings. That is, partners listen to each other simply to pick points to attack rather than to understand the other person's perspective.

3. Emotional distance and isolation

When a trust issue arises in a relationship where trust doesn't already exist, there is nothing partners can rely on as leverage. This leads them to shutting down emotionally and distancing themselves from each other.

Signs of Trust Issues

In the section above, we looked at how lack of trust can quickly sprout issues within a relationship. While some partners try to prevent these issues, they usually can't recognize them when they surface. So, this section aims to show how trust issues manifest in relationships so you can identify them better.

Trust issues manifest differently in every relationship. While some partners may easily get jealous or worried their partner might be cheating on them, others struggle to believe their partners' words and actions are genuine. So, it's important to determine if your feelings are not consequences of a deep-rooted problem.

That said, look out for the following behavioral patterns to know whether you or your partner has trust issues:

1. High likelihood to blame or overreact

If you're quick to blame your partner or vice versa, overreact, or constantly look for signs of infidelity, this is a sign of a trust issue. You tend to exhibit this behavior when you think your partner might hurt or abandon you.

2. Commitment issues

If you would rather your partner keep their distance than stay close to you, that might be a sign of trust issues. The reason you struggle to commit to them might be that you fear they may not be trustworthy.

3. Attraction to mistrustful partners

There is a high tendency for you to develop trust issues when you get together with a partner whose way is wayward. When your partner cheats, for instance, it is hard to trust them.

How to Overcome Trust Issues

Trust issues in a relationship usually lead to emotional disconnection. It's like a thorn in the foot; it will keep hurting if you don't remove it. That's why it's not enough to recognize trust issues; we must also explore how you can overcome them, and below are some steps to guide you:

1. Express your feelings

When you openly communicate your insecurities to your partner rather than bottle them up, it helps them understand what you are going through and creates room for an open conversation. Herein, you can discuss what triggers your trust issues and how you can tackle them.

2. Rebuild the trust with small steps

Sometimes, all you need is to take it slowly. If your trust in your partner has been broken, you could patch it up by starting with small acts until it's all fixed.

3. Seek to understand first before being understood

Often, try to put yourself in other people's shoes and be empathetic toward their plight. This way, you create a safe space for them to discuss the things bothering them, thereby creating room for trust.

How to Build and Maintain Trust

Once you discover an opportunity to build or repair trust with your partner, make it your top priority to begin working on it immediately. Now, you may be confused about how exactly to go about this, which is why I've curated simple steps to help you build and maintain trust in your relationship:

1. Talk to each other.
2. Listen sympathetically and try to be present with your partner.
3. Ask questions to better understand them.

4. Say what you mean and mean what you say.
5. Find ways to connect with your partner.
6. Be willing to work on areas where your relationship could improve.
7. Create positive experiences together.

When Trust Is Broken

Sometimes, you might manage to build trust with your partner, only for something to mess it all up, and you have to start all over again. Whether it was entirely or partly your fault or not your fault at all, rebuilding trust can be pretty challenging. Nonetheless, here are some easy ways to rebuild trust more effectively:

1. Pick up the pieces

Look for where the main instigator of the broken trust came from. Identify, review and assess this particular issue and look for solutions. Afterward, you can pick up the pieces of your love that the issue has broken and mend it together. Still remember Kintsugi?

2. Know the details

Ensure that the offending partner explains themself, giving a clearer perspective on what caused the issue. If you don't take the time to analyze the details, you will struggle with the solutions.

3. Release the anger

I don't mean you should lash at your partner when you have an issue with them. You can quickly rebuild trust between your partner by reflecting on the anger and letting it go after clarifying the issue and how you can solve it.

Stop the Blame Game and Start Taking Responsibility

People find it easy to throw complaints and blame around carelessly but are less inclined to talk about the solutions to the problem. However, it's important to start taking responsibility to promote trust between you and your partner. And you can do this by different means.

How to Take Accountability

Taking accountability for what you did is a pretty challenging task. Not only do you acknowledge the conflict, but you also admit your role in it. However, holding yourself accountable is easier when you involve your partner. For instance, talking to your partner about improving your relationship will make you more conscious about how your actions affect others.

Similarly, you can take accountability by looking through your regular behaviors either by yourself or with your partner. Then take time to look through some common problems in your relationship. Try to see if any of your regular behaviors aren't instigators of these problems. If they are, take accountability by considering how these behaviors influence the problems and how you can improve.

However, if the process becomes too overwhelming, or you find yourself stuck on what to do, pause and take a breather, then consider involving a third party such as a therapist. Sometimes, you need the guidance of a professional to learn accountability.

Avoiding the Blame Game

People don't throw blame around because they enjoy doing so; it's just easier to point out others' faults than it is to point out ours. Throwing blame carelessly may be a fast way to win an argument, but it's also a quick way to lose your relationship. Thus, you must be careful and avoid the blame game. Below are ten steps that can guide you through how to stop the blame game and start to see what works well in your relationship:

- Put yourself in your partner's shoes.
- Talk about things that are bothering you.
- Listen actively to your partner.
- Focus on the things you have control over.
- Talk about your roles with each other.
- Let some things go; not everything is worth fighting over.
- Don't take it personally.
- Think about your actions and whether you deserve to be blamed instead.
- Get professional help if the issue persists.

Intimacy

The word "intimacy" comes from the Latin word "intimus," which means "innermost." Therefore, when we talk about intimacy, we talk about how partners bond with each other on many levels. An even more interesting definition of intimacy is the "blending of hearts." It is that emotional feature that allows you to see into your partner and vice versa.

However, intimacy can mean different things to people in their relationships because of the various ways it manifests. Hence, we'll look at five types and how they concern your relationship:

- **Intellectual intimacy:** This intimacy is built when you are on the same wavelength as your partner, so you understand each other so much through your intellectual prowess.
- **Emotional intimacy:** This is the most common type of intimacy. It is the intimacy you develop by expressing and satisfying a strong need to be close to each other.
- **Spiritual intimacy:** Some partners also bond over shared spiritual beliefs. These are the kind of people who believe that their meeting their partner isn't by accident, but by a spiritual power.

- **Sexual intimacy:** This is developed through the freedom to express yourself to your partner sexually. And it goes beyond having sex; it is also about you giving a part of yourself to your partner.
- **Mutual intimacy:** Herein, partners maturely show intimacy, allowing each other to create a space where their differences are recognized and they work towards solving them.

The Importance of Intimacy

Intimacy between partners brings so many benefits to their relationship, which makes intimacy a non-negotiable quality in every relationship. The following are just a few other reasons why intimacy is so important in a relationship:

- It builds trust and security.
- It enhances communication.
- It creates a sense of safety.
- It allows for the sharing of emotions without judgment.
- It allows for open and honest conversations between partners.

How to Increase Intimacy in Your Relationship

Now that we've talked about why intimacy is so important for strengthening your relationship, let's dive into what you can do to keep it strong. And if your connection with your partner starts to dwindle, here are some ways to increase the level of intimacy in your relationship:

1. Try something new

When you do something every single day, it is only a matter of time before it loses its quality. This is why you have to try out something new and unexpected every now and then to reignite the spark and keep your relationship interesting.

2. Reminisce

Learn to talk about the good times you've shared with your partner. When you remind them about a beautiful memory like a fun park you both visited, it helps take them back in time to that period, increasing their desire to have that feeling again.

3. Schedule sex

You are legally married, so sex should strengthen and not weaken your intimacy with your partner. Scheduling sex with your partner provides you both with that opportunity to build anticipation, which engages the brain itself directly.

4. Stay connected

Don't forget to check on your partner throughout the day. Even if you are at the office, you can stay connected with them through texts. This lets them know they matter a lot to you.

5. Go on a date

Bring back the juice all over again and go on dates with them. Choose a comfortable and quiet venue where you both can talk without being disturbed.

Questions That Build Intimacy

If you start to feel distant from your partner, set a time for you two to ask thought-provoking questions. But before you ask any questions, you and your partner should agree not to give polar answers; that means it's not enough to simply say "yes" or "no." This way, you can have a deeper conversation and discover the root problem. This is a list of some questions couples can ask one another:

1. What's something you're hesitant to share with anyone else?
2. What were three things about me that initially attracted you to me?
3. When did you realize you loved me?
4. Describe your ideal day.

5. What's something you've always wanted to ask me but haven't?
6. What have I done that made you proud, and when was it?
7. What's your biggest regret?
8. If you could relive one day in our relationship, which day would it be?
9. What do you enjoy most about our physical connection, and how could we make it even better?
10. Which of the five senses do you find most sensual?

Reigniting the Spark

You might have tried everything discussed in the sections above, but the spark that used to exist in your relationship remains dead for a reason you can't figure out. If it's any comfort, you *can* rekindle a dying or dead relationship. Even more, the process is very simple to follow.

1. Bring back the date nights

Try setting aside a night once or twice a week to go out on a date with your partner and see how much change you get to see in the relationship. All you need to do is make sure that whatever day and time you choose is comfortable for you both, not a time when either or the two of you are engaged in something else.

2. Communicate

Once you settle into the warmth of comfort, you may easily forget the need to talk to your partners about how you feel. So, to reignite the spark, try communicating more consistently. Create time to not only share your feelings with your partners but also to listen to them actively.

3. Recognize them

In a way, everyone seeks validation. People want to be seen, appreciated, and recognized, so don't deny your partner this craving.

When you hesitate to acknowledge their efforts, it hurts your intimacy in the long run.

Interactive Element

We have explored the concept of trust and intimacy extensively. It is time to check for yourself how much of these qualities you possess by taking the test crafted by Lewicki & Wiethoff below:

Create free time when you and your partner are both comfortable with and disengaged from other activities. Print this out on a sheet of paper and pass a copy to them. Both of you should read the questions well and ensure that your answers are completely honest.

1. What is trust to you?
2. When was a time when trust was broken in one of your relationships?
3. What were the circumstances surrounding the trust being broken?
4. What were your thoughts and feelings in the aftermath of the trust being broken?
5. What role did you play in the trust being broken?
6. What could you have done differently to prevent the trust from breaking?
7. What steps can you take to rebuild trust in this relationship?
8. How can you avoid similar trust issues in future relationships?

Starting Your Own Rituals

Once you have properly assessed the answers and determined what works for both of you, engage in these three rituals to further create a better connection between you both:

1. Create a moment of reunion

Interact with your partner every day. People tend to lose that sense of excitement when the daily greeting or validation ritual is broken, so try your best to be consistent.

2. Set aside at least two minutes of communication without distraction

Within these two minutes, nothing else should take priority over your discussion or interaction with your partner. I only suggested two minutes so you don't feel overwhelmed starting out, but if you can go the extra mile, feel free to.

3. Practice appreciation

Always appreciate the good that your partner does to you. Most couples tend to take their partner's good actions for granted, and it often doesn't create the excitement they need to foster intimacy.

In this chapter, we've explored the foundations of trust and intimacy, diving into what it takes to create and sustain a safe and open relationship. By focusing on mutual understanding, communication, and genuine connection, we open the door to a partnership where two partners can find the strength to grow, heal, and rebuild — together. However, in the next chapter, we will explore how building intimacy with your partner prepares you for mutual growth with them.

Chapter SEVEN

THRIVING TOGETHER TODAY AND EVERY DAY

> *"In the arithmetic of love, one plus one equals everything, and two minus one equals nothing."*
>
> **— Mignon McLaughlin**

The love story of Johnny Cash and June Carter has lived rent-free in the minds of country music fans for decades. The duo first crossed paths in 1956 when Cash performed at the Grand Ole Opry. Around this time, Carter was married to Carl Smith, while Cash was married to Viviane Liberto. By the early 1960s, Cash and Carter had already begun touring together. However, life for the two wasn't without its challenges. Carter, for one, had divorced her first husband Smith and remarried Edwin Nix, while Cash was battling with addictions to drugs and alcohol, causing him to cancel or entirely miss out on shows and concerts. As far as society was concerned, these two were nothing but broken records.

Fast forward to 1966, Cash's marriage to Viviane Liberto was on the rocks, later leading to divorce due to his addictions and reported infidelity. Coincidentally, Carter's second marriage to Edwin Nix also ended that same year.

However, as Cash and Carter continued their tours, they developed strong feelings for each other. Then, two years later, Johnny Cash proposed to June Carter in front of a live audience on stage in London, Ontario. The duo got married just a few weeks later, but that's not the best part of this love story. The best part is that Carter helped Cash get sober, transforming the rebellious country crooner into a distinguished Man in Black. Little wonder why, on June Carter's 65th birthday, when their love had grown so old, Johnny could still write her this heartfelt letter:

"You still fascinate and inspire me. You influence me for the better. You're the object of my desire, the #1 Earthly reason for my existence. We got old and got used to each other. We think alike. We read each other's minds. We know what the other wants without asking. Sometimes, we irritate each other a little bit. Maybe we take each other for granted. But once in a while, like today, I meditate on it and realize how lucky I am to share my life with the greatest woman I ever met."

Their love for each other was so strong that when June Carter passed away in May 2003 at the age of 73, Johnny Cash joined her less than four months later. Cash and Carter's love story is one of legacy and emulation to the whole world. Even after their passing, their story still touches the hearts of fans near and far, inspiring everyone to choose to support our partners by being there for them through adversities. The only way to do that is by spending a lot of quality time with them. For instance, when asked about Carter's definition of paradise, he replied, "This morning with her having coffee", reflecting how intimate you can get with your partner simply by being there with them.

Love stories as beautiful as this one don't happen accidentally. So much intentional effort goes on behind the scenes. We can only imagine how much work it took Carter to help her husband navigate through his chronic addictions. This reflects that a beautiful love story often has ugly efforts behind it.

Why Relationships Take Work

Many of us believe our soulmates are somewhere waiting for us and that at the right time, they will appear like an angel, and we will fall madly in love with them, get married to them, and have kids with them. We believe this person will be perfect and meet our expectations, so we will definitely live happily ever after. I hate to break it to you, but life isn't like a Disney fairytale. All relationships require work, attention, patience and tolerance to work out successfully.

Relationships take hard work to succeed for various reasons, including the differences between you and your partner. When you read Cash and Carter's love story, it's clear that Cash was such a wayward husband that Vivianne couldn't help but leave. It must have taken so much work for Carter to help him change (something Cash's first wife couldn't do).

Another reason relationships take hard work to succeed is that long-lasting relationships require mutual effort. Unless two partners are willing to make sacrifices to sustain their relationship, their relationship will suffer.

Boundless Love Entails Respecting Boundaries

A boundary is a clear line of demarcation that informs you where to stop. It can define where one thing ends and where another one begins. When it comes to relationships, boundaries define where things like our personhood, identity, responsibility, and control begin and end when it comes to our partner. And although boundaries sound like a way to create distance between you and your partner, this is far from true. They serve a crucial role in maintaining your identity and promoting your physical well-being, which all tend to have a lasting effect on your overall interaction with your partner in the end.

There are several types of boundaries in relationships that sometimes overlap. Here are some of them:

Physical relationship boundaries

This includes the lines you draw regarding how you care for your body and physical environment. It revolves around how you prefer to be touched, what should be in your personal space, and your physical needs.

Emotional relationship boundaries

These boundaries protect your right to feel and think a certain way without being criticized or dismissed by your partner.

Sexual relationship boundaries

With these boundaries, you tell your partner what you are willing to do and are comfortable with in your sex life and what you might not readily want to try out. It can revolve around touch, sight, and the way you want to be treated in a sexual context.

Financial relationship boundaries

These boundaries dictate how someone prefers to manage their finances. For instance, your partner may advocate against the idea of setting up a joint account. This means they have financial boundaries regarding how they want to spend their own money. Financial boundaries can also extend to how much you're willing to spend or on what things.

Why You Need Boundaries

It doesn't matter what kind of relationship you have with someone — whether they're your romantic partner, relative, friend, or coworker — boundaries help you avoid conflicts.

A study shows that when boundaries are blurred between personal life and work, people experience more emotional burnout and less happiness. However, not all boundaries are advisable, so knowing the difference between healthy and unhealthy boundaries is important.

Healthy vs Unhealthy Boundaries

Generally, we refer to it as a healthy boundary when you create a boundary that helps maintain your well-being and ensures your physical and emotional safety. But those boundaries that weigh on your overall well-being and threaten your physical and emotional safety are the unhealthy ones you should avoid. Usually, some boundaries may appear healthy on the surface until you assess them and realize they aren't. Below are some examples of healthy and unhealthy boundaries in a relationship to help you easily recognize them:

Examples of healthy boundaries

- Communicating your needs and expectations with others and being open to theirs.
- Leaving a situation that makes you feel uncomfortable and unsafe.
- Taking time for self-care, even if it means turning down invitations or requests from people.
- Saying no without fear of rejection or worry of being viewed negatively.
- Expressing your beliefs and views rather than downplaying them.

Examples of unhealthy boundaries

- Asking people to always say yes to you to prove they are good friends.
- Asking someone to change their interests to suit yours.
- Asking your partner to always be available in case you want to spend time with them or asking them to forgo their activities.
- Forcing your partner to do something sexual, even when it makes them uncomfortable.

Signs You Need Better Boundaries

There are times you experience a mental or physical breakdown and lodge the blame on how much work you have done at the office or on how much someone has stressed you. Sometimes, you may not consider others' needs when setting boundaries. Other times, you may struggle to determine whether or not your boundaries are effective. The truth is, deciding whether or not to revise your boundaries can be tricky, but it doesn't have to be that way. Once you notice the signs below, see them as a cue that you need to set better boundaries:

1. Burnout

When you always say yes to others' requests, even when they don't align with your needs or situation, you'll easily get burned out. However, it's important to know when to draw the line and say no, even when it's your partner.

2. Resentment

This is usually a consequence of burnout. When a request emotionally drains you, you tend to break down and take out the anger on your partner, blaming them for crossing a boundary you never set in the first place.

3. Anxiety

When someone requests something from you, there is this mental anxiety that immediately grows in your mind the next time you see them or receive either a call or text from them. This anxiety is a sign that you need to create a better boundary.

How to Set and Enforce Boundaries

You've learned what a boundary is, its types, and what constitutes a healthy and unhealthy boundary. But we haven't answered the most important question: How do you set healthy boundaries in your relationship to help it grow?

First, it is important to know what you need from your relationship by being clear about the kind of person you are with, their needs, and whether they are being met. It would also help if you learned to practice healthy communication. You can do this by communicating your thoughts, feelings, and needs to your partner and requesting that they be met in the relationship.

Furthermore, you must ensure you choose the right time to discuss boundaries with your partner. Certain issues have certain periods in which they need to be discussed. For instance, asking to know your partner should always come at the beginning of the relationship. However, for boundaries, raise them at specific points in time when they are relevant to the situation.

Harnessing the Power of Vulnerability

Vulnerability is an integral ingredient of a lasting relationship, but often, we find it hard to open up to our partners. Even though we seek intimacy, we are often afraid of being seen and exposed, so we cover ourselves with a blanket of deception. However, vulnerability has so many benefits to offer in a relationship.

One of these benefits is that it increases the chances of meeting our needs. When you dare to ask for what you truly want, you might later end up getting it. But when you don't, the answer is automatically and always no, and your desire may never be satisfied.

Another benefit is that when you start advocating for your needs, you begin to feel better about yourself, improving your sense of authenticity and worthiness. Vulnerability also builds trust in relationships. When you show your partner that you are not always strong and that there are times your softer side manifests, it gives them the room to accept you as a human, increasing their faith in you.

More on Vulnerability

At this point, you might be wondering, *How can I be more vulnerable?* Simply put, you start by sharing how you feel with your partner. Although this sounds basic on the surface, it is harder to practice. Being vulnerable might mean telling your partner what goes on in your mind or how your day went. This may include going to work and coming back home to tell them how stressful work was, or how interesting your colleagues were that day.

Sometimes, you can also be more vulnerable with your partner by explaining to them how or why something has annoyed you. This will help you avoid the temptation to be passive-aggressive with anger, resort to using negative comments, or become distant.

However, vulnerability isn't for you alone; you can also invite your partner to be more vulnerable with you through such exercises like revealing yourselves, walking straight into fear, and coming out of hiding — all of which will be explained in the couples' exercise soon. However, before you can invite your partner to be vulnerable with you, you must be vulnerable with them first. Once they sense that you are always willing to open up when you are not fine, it makes it easier for them to do the same.

Opening Up

In this section, I'll provide some instructions to help you get the hang of being vulnerable. However, note that these exercises will be divided into two parts: individual exercise and couple exercise.

Individual Exercises

As an individual striving to be more vulnerable with their partner, you must understand that the work starts with you. Before you can invite your partner to practice this vulnerability with you, you need to have started first yourself. And to start, you could begin with:

Doing Something That Scares You

This is a pretty straightforward and simple thing to do. Everyone of us has those things that scare us, and as a consequence, it can hold us back from reaching our full potential with our partners. Therefore, to practice vulnerability, you could start with doing something that scares you. Go skydiving. Tell that honest truth you've always kept from your partner. Tell them about wanting a kid. Just do something.

Vulnerability Prompts

Similarly, you can engage in some vulnerability prompts by taking any of these exercises at intervals, or randomly. They include:

Word Association Exercise

On a blank page, write the word "vulnerable" at the top. Below it, jot down the first word that comes to mind. Keep writing one word after another, without pausing or censoring your thoughts, until your mind feels quiet and no more words come to you. When you're done, review your list. What interesting connections stand out? Do you notice any patterns? What insights about yourself can you draw from this exercise?

Freewriting on Vulnerability

Spend ten minutes writing freely about what it means to feel vulnerable.

Reflecting on Vulnerability

Think about a time when you felt most vulnerable. What happened? Was the experience positive or negative? How has it shaped the way you respond to vulnerability now?

Feeling Invulnerable

Reflect on when you feel the least vulnerable, most protected, strong, or invincible. Do you feel more or less connected to others during these times? Freewrite for ten minutes about your thoughts.

Listing Types of Vulnerability

Create a list of different types of vulnerability, interpreted in any way that makes sense to you. Which type makes your relationship feel more emotionally charged? Why?

Couple Exercise

To ensure vulnerability between both you and your partner, three different exercises are recommended for you to ease your partner into being more vulnerable with you. If you intend to do them all, then it is more effective when they are done in the order with which they appear.

Exercise 1: Revealing Yourself

1. Set a timer for five minutes.
2. Sit facing your partner.
3. Make eye contact with them.
4. Take a moment to settle into your connection with your partner and observe your feelings for a few seconds.
5. Partner 1 should begin by saying: "Being with you, I notice ________," and share whatever comes up — thoughts, feelings, sensations, or beliefs.
6. Partner 2 should listen and let it sink in. Then, respond with: "Hearing that, I notice ________," sharing their inner experience.
7. Partner 1 listens, lets it land, and responds: "Hearing that, I notice ________," sharing their inner experience again."
8. Continue alternating responses (steps 6 and 7) until the timer goes off.
9. Reflect on the experience — what was it like for each of you?

Exercise 2: Walking Straight into Fear

1. Set a 10-minute timer.
2. Sit facing your partner.
3. Maintain eye contact.
4. Take a moment to connect and notice how you feel.
5. Partner 1 begins by saying, "The thing I'm most afraid to say right now is ____________."
6. If needed, take time to process what was shared.
7. Partner 2 then shares, "The thing I'm most afraid to say right now is ____________."
8. Process their response if necessary.
9. Continue alternating steps 5–8 until the timer ends.

Exercise 3: Coming out of Hiding

1. Sit facing your partner.
2. Maintain eye contact.
3. Take a moment to connect and tune into your feelings.

4. Partner 1 answers, "What are the ways you avoid being fully seen?" and shares for 90 seconds.
5. Partner 1 answers, "What parts of you are you afraid to be seen?" and shares for 90 seconds.
6. While maintaining eye contact, Partner 1 embodies one of the parts that feels afraid to be seen. For 90 seconds, fully experience, express, and even speak from that part, allowing your partner to witness it.
7. Pause to process and reflect on the experience together.
8. Switch roles and repeat steps 4–7.

Cultivating the Attitude of Gratitude

According to Dr. John Gottman, there are seven principles for keeping a relationship strong, and it is no mistake that appreciation sits at number two. This is because gratitude helps build and maintain relationships by focusing on people's positive aspects. Also, because gratitude has waned so much in the present society and has been replaced with disappointment, anger, and resentment, it doesn't go unnoticed when you shower your partner with it.

Scientific Studies on the Power of Gratitude

Research from the University of Georgia highlights the importance of expressing affection and gratitude in relationships. In the study, couples were interviewed about how appreciated and valued they felt by their spouse. Professor Ted Futris, one of the study's authors, explained, "Our findings show that feeling valued and appreciated by your partner directly impacts how satisfied you are with your marriage, how committed you feel, and your confidence in its longevity."

Psychologist Amie Gordon from the University of California, Berkeley, has also extensively studied the impact of gratitude on our lives, providing valuable insights for enhancing romantic relationships. According to Gordon, feelings of gratitude toward a romantic partner could predict relationship longevity. "We discovered that participants who expressed greater gratitude were more likely to remain in their relationships nine months later," she explained.

Thoughtful Ways to Express Gratitude

Now that you know how important gratitude is in your relationship, you need to know the effective ways to express gratitude to your partner. Below are just a few ways you can go about it:

- **Send a card:** Writing a heartfelt message to your partner is a thoughtful way to show you care about them.
- **Make small kind gestures:** Thoughtful actions, like bringing home their favorite treat or watching a show they love, can strengthen your connection and show you're thinking of them.
- **Practice active listening:** Give your partner your full attention during conversations. Avoid multitasking and create a space where they feel safe to share openly, even about difficult topics, as noted by Farmer-Brackett, a clinical training manager at Centerstone.
- **Lend a hand:** If your partner seems overwhelmed, step in to lighten their load by tackling tasks they dislike, like taking out the trash.
- **Offer genuine compliments:** Show appreciation with a specific and heartfelt compliment, such as "You're always so good at (specific task or trait)."

Beyond these steps, you can also express gratitude to your partner through the following exercises:

Gratitude Journal

Explore pre-made couples' journals or create your own to bring that writing practice into your relationship. Writing love letters can be a fun and meaningful activity to express gratitude.

Three things before bed

End each day by sharing three specific things you appreciate about your partner. This simple practice, recommended by a therapist, develops connection and gratitude.

Have a giving week

Set aside days to give your partner random gifts to acknowledge their efforts. It makes them feel seen and appreciated, too.

Opening Your Mind to Other Forms of Help

Throughout this book, we have explored different ways you can easily navigate the complexities of your relationship, but sometimes, your relationship might need much more. That's why you need to learn to open your mind to other solutions, especially couple therapy.

Benefits of Couples Therapy

There's a popular stereotype that couples therapy is meant only for those partners who are struggling with their relationship, but that's not true. Any couple can enjoy the benefits of therapy, whether they're struggling or not. Below are some of these benefits:

1. It helps improve the communication skills between partners.
2. It creates a safe space for both partners to thrive and trust each other.
3. It guides you toward building understanding and empathy in your relationship.
4. It helps you navigate conflicts in the right way.
5. It helps you work through life's challenges.

Signs You Should Give Therapy a Try

Many partners tend to think their relationship is doing just fine, even when it is falling apart pretty fast. As a result, you need to know what signs in a relationship call for the urgent need for couples therapy.

One of these signs is dwindling intimacy between you and your partner. When you start to notice that you and your partner are falling out and nothing is changing, no matter your efforts, you should immediately give therapy a try.

Another sign you might need couples therapy is the fear of communicating with each other. Communication is key in every long-lasting relationship. So, when it becomes lost between couples, there is an urgent need to seek help from therapy.

Also, when you notice that the trust you and your partner have in each other starts dissipating, know that your relationship is at risk. Do not hesitate to reach out to a professional for help immediately.

What to Expect from Couples Therapy

Couple therapists often take an integrated approach to treatment, borrowing solutions across different forms of therapy depending on your needs. Usually, they may take the following strategies:

- Getting to know you
- Identifying your feelings
- Exploring your past
- Focusing on what solutions apply to your needs

Relationship Check-Ins

Relationship check-ins can often help you understand and solve issues in your relationship before the need for couples therapy arises. They involve dedicating a specific time to discussing the state of your relationship with your partner. The conversation will revolve solely around the relationship and nothing more.

To do this, you need to start by introducing the idea of a check-in to your partner. Then, you find a time and location where it will be regularly held. After this, ensure you have gotten rid of all forms of distractions that may arise and treat the time as sacred. Throughout the conversation, be mindful of how you speak to avoid arguments, and always remember to focus on solutions rather than the problems.

To further assess the state of your relationship with your partner, engage in this exercise crafted into insightful questions. Ensure to ask your partner these questions and jot down their responses.

1. Reflect on the past week; can you identify when you felt especially valued and cared for in our relationship?
2. What three aspects of our relationship do you treasure most right now, and why are they so important to you?
3. Were there any moments this week you felt overlooked or taken for granted? What can we do to avoid that in the future?
4. What positive shifts have you noticed in our relationship over the past week?
5. In what ways did I show my appreciation for you, and how did it strengthen our bond?
6. How can I better acknowledge and show gratitude for the small things you do each week?
7. What small actions or gestures I might not have noticed but could make you feel more loved and valued this week?

Interactive Element

Whether your marriage feels strong or is going through challenges, there's always room for growth. To help you nurture your relationship, here is a list of twenty-eight ways to invest in your marriage. Take on this challenge, commit to each one, and watch your marriage thrive.

Day 1: Send a thankful text to your partner, expressing gratitude for their actions. Even if it's difficult, try to focus on the positives.

Day 2: Do a small act of service, like completing one of their usual chores to make their day easier.

Day 3: Leave a thoughtful note somewhere they'll easily find it, like in the bathroom mirror or between the pages of a book they're reading.

Day 4: Call them during the day just to say you love them — no agenda, just a sweet surprise.

Day 5: Gift them a small surprise, like their favorite snack, to show you're thinking of them.

Day 6: Let go of minor annoyances today and focus on the qualities you love about your partner.

Day 7: Send them an inspiring or meaningful quote that reflects your feelings for them.

Day 8: Plan a surprise lunch date. If you have kids, get creative, like meeting at a park.

Day 9: Dress up for your partner as a reminder of your attractiveness to them.

Day 10: Send a flirty or romantic text to let them know you desire them.

Day 11: Take the initiative in intimacy to show your partner how much you want them.

Day 12: Treat them to a relaxing back massage.

Day 13: Play a game you both enjoy and share some fun and laughter.

Day 14: Take a walk together for exercise and meaningful conversation.

Day 15: Surprise them with breakfast in bed.

Day 16: Try something new together, like a class or activity, to create shared experiences.

Day 17: Share a song that expresses your feelings for them.

Day 18: Write down ten things you love about your partner and give it to them.

Day 19: Cook or order their favorite meal.

Day 20: Recreate your first date for a nostalgic and romantic evening.

Day 21: Laugh together by sharing funny videos or clips.

Day 22: Give them several heartfelt compliments throughout the day.

Day 23: Have a "dream date" where you talk about your future aspirations together.

Day 24: Spend time just making out to reignite intimacy.

Day 25: Send a cute selfie — bonus points if it's flirty or cheeky.

Day 26: Write a heartfelt love letter to express your feelings.

Day 27: Go shopping and choose something you know they'd look great in.

Day 28: Do something you know they'll love, like a small task or gesture that means a lot to them.

In summary, we have explored the importance of being there for each other every day in a relationship, including helping a relationship thrive. We also discussed the importance of boundaries, vulnerability, gratitude, couples therapy, and relationship check-ins. Essentially, building a resilient relationship takes showing up for each other day after day. But before we wrap things up, let's consider how these habits we have discussed can keep you and your partner on a path of shared growth, love, and happiness.

CONCLUSION

At the beginning of this book, you learned how important you are in communication. We did this by discussing self-awareness and why you need to know yourself before you can communicate effectively. We also discussed the importance of emotional intelligence, using it as a bridge to reach your partner by discerning how they respond to your interactions. Then, we looked into empathy as a significant part of communication. This is because when you don't see things from your partner's perspective in an interaction, you might struggle to understand them. The only way to understand someone is to take the time to listen to them.

The journey to effective communication solely rests on active listening. As we have established in Chapter 2, communication doesn't occur until someone is on the receiving end. This reflects how important it is for you and your partner to pay more attention to what the other person is saying rather than be quick to respond. This isn't limited to their verbal responses, as we have seen in the book; it can also be extended to their body language, such as their sitting posture and facial expressions. For instance, a smile during an interaction can easily suggest that your partner is happy about what you're saying. And this somewhat foregrounds how effective language is regarding emotional bonding.

Language is that bridge you need to reach your partner, but you can't get to the other side of the bridge until you make conscious efforts to move. These conscious efforts concerning language include understanding that your partner has a love language and finding a way to adapt to it. Don't just recognize your partner's love language; speak it.

Now, the essence of understanding your partner's needs and working toward fulfilling them is that it helps you avoid conflicts in your relationship. Although conflicts will always happen since anger is natural due to people's differences, you can easily manage it by understanding what your partner needs in your relationship. When you ignore the solutions instead and fight their anger with anger, you will hardly resolve anything.

Therefore, to ensure that you don't fall into the pit of destroying your love life from an emotional breakdown, this book also provides detailed steps on the techniques you can use to regulate your emotions. These techniques include breathwork exercises, guided meditation, body scan, visualization, and progressive muscle relaxation, among others.

In essence, you have learned from this book that a number of the problems that arise in relationships, including misunderstanding, conflicts, resentment, emotional distance, stonewalling, contempt, and decreased intimacy, can all be tied to a lack of proper communication. When effective communication is breached between partners, they can't get anything across to each other. This book has not only shown you how important communication is but also how to be a better communicator in your relationship.

So, are you ready to build a love-centered connection with your partner? Leverage the CONNECT framework and take your first step toward the relationship you have always dreamt of — starting today!

PS: If this book taught you something new or helped you better understand and be understood by your partner, then help someone else revive their relationship by leaving us a review. Thank you!

REFERENCES

10 Communication Mistakes Made in Every Relationship - Relish. (n.d.). Relish. https://hellorelish.com/articles/communication-mistakes-in-relationships.html

10 Ways to Show Your Partner Appreciation. (2023, September 27). Centerstone. https://centerstone.org/our-resources/health-wellness/10-ways-to-show-your-partner-appreciation/

11 Phrases You Should Avoid When Arguing With Your Partner. (2023). Couply. https://www.couply.io/post/phrases-you-should-avoid-when-arguing-with-your-partner

52 Romantic Questions For Getting to Know Your Partner Better - Relish. (n.d.). Relish. https://hellorelish.com/articles/romantic-questions-to-ask-your-partner.html

Abramson, A. (2021, November 1). *Cultivating Empathy.* American Psychological Association. https://www.apa.org/monitor/2021/11/feature-cultivating-empathy

Ackerman, C. (2017, December 18). *87 self-reflection questions for introspection [+exercises].* PositivePsychology. https://positivepsychology.com/introspection-self-reflection/

Ackerman, C. (2020, April 1). *What is Self-Awareness and Why is it Important? [+5 Ways to Increase It].* PositivePsychology. https://positivepsychology.com/self-awareness-matters-how-you-can-be-more-self-aware/

Aithor. (2024, June 3). *The Importance of Trust in a Relationship.* Aithor. https://aithor.com/essay-examples/the-importance-of-trust-in-a-relationship

Alispahic, S. (2023, July 15). *Rebuilding Trust In A Relationship Worksheet | HappierTHERAPY.* HappierTherapy.

https://happiertherapy.com/rebuilding-trust-in-a-relationship-worksheet/

Anderson, C. (2022, March 12). *Top Things Couples Fight About | Minneapolis Psychiatrists*. Innovative Psychological Consultants. https://www.ipc-mn.com/what-are-the-top-three-things-couples-fight-about

Applying The 5 Love Languages™ to healthy relationships. (n.d.). Love Is Respect. https://www.loveisrespect.org/resources/applying-the-5-love-languages-to-healthy-relationships/

A quote by Alain de Botton. (n.d.). Goodreads. https://www.goodreads.com/quotes/538989-intimacy-is-the-capacity-to-be-rather-weird-with-someone

A quote by Ambrose Bierce. (n.d.). Goodreads. https://www.goodreads.com/quotes/9909-speak-when-you-are-angry-and-you-will-make-the

Banks, D. (2024, May 13). *10 Differences in Healthy vs Unhealthy Fighting in Relationships*. Marriage.com. https://www.marriage.com/advice/relationship/healthy-fighting-vs-unhealthy-fighting/

Barnes, M. (2021, March 17). *6 Active Listening Activities for Couples*. Body+Mind Magazine. https://bodymind.com/6-active-listening-activities-for-couples/

Benefits of Going to Couples Therapy. (2021, July 6). Advanced Psychiatry Associates. https://advancedpsychiatryassociates.com/resources/blog/benefits-of-couples-therapy

BetterHelp Editorial Team. (2019, July 7). *The 5 Love Languages: How To Show Love To Your Partner | BetterHelp*. BetterHelp. https://www.betterhelp.com/advice/love/the-5-love-languages-how-to-show-love-to-your-partner/

Brady, K. (2019, July 31). *10 Ways To Increase Intimacy In Your Relationship*. Keir Brady Counseling Services. https://keir-bradycounseling.com/10-ways-to-increase-intimacy/

Campbell, K. (2017, November 2). *The Importance of Gratitude in Relationships*. Bayview Therapy. https://www.bayviewtherapy.com/single-post/the-importance-of-gratitude-in-relationships

Carpenter, D. (2024). How to Develop Empathy in Relationships. VeryWell Mind. https://www.verywellmind.com/how-to-develop-empathy-in-relationships-1717547

Chapman, G. (n.d.). *The Five Love Languages Test*. https://nbcgutah.com/wp-content/uploads/2017/09/5.LoveLanguageTest.pdf

Chung, M. (2023, August 29). *When to Go to Couples Therapy: 13 Signs It's Time*. Talkspace. https://www.talkspace.com/blog/signs-you-need-to-go-to-couples-therapy/

Cleveland Clinic. (2023, May 25). *7 Ways To Improve Your Active Listening Skills*. Cleveland Clinic. https://health.clevelandclinic.org/active-listening

Cooks-Campbell, A. (2021, August 19). *Breathwork: The Secret to Emotional Regulation*. BetterUp. https://www.betterup.com/blog/breathwork

Cooks-Campbell, A. (2023, February 8). *8 Types of Nonverbal Communication That Can Help to Improve Your Speech*. BetterUp. https://www.betterup.com/blog/types-of-nonverbal-communication

Couple Summit Team. (2021, September 13). *Relationship Check-ins: Why They Matter and Questions To Ask for Relationship Health*. Couple Summit. https://www.thecouplesummit.org/blog/relationship-check-ins

Cronkleton, E. (2019, April 9). *10 Breathing Techniques*. Healthline. https://www.healthline.com/health/breathing-exercise

Danny. (2021, November 14). *The Definition of Trust in a Relationship*. Happily Committed. https://happilycommitted.com/definition-of-trust-in-a-relationship/

Deering, S. (2023, April 20). *35 Simple, Sincere Phrases To Express Empathy*. Parade. https://parade.com/living/empathy-statements

Department of Communication, Indiana State University. (n.d.). 4.2 Listening Styles. *Whatcom Community College*. https://textbooks.whatcom.edu/duttoncmst101/chapter/listening-styles/

editor. (2023, July 19). *The role of Emotional Intelligence in Effective Communication [5 Roles]*. Rcademy. https://rcademy.com/role-of-emotional-intelligence-in-effective-communication/

Eikenberry, K. (2022, August 31). *The 10 Questions You Need to Be a Better Listener - The Kevin Eikenberry Group*. The Kevin Eikenberry Group. https://kevineikenberry.com/communication-interpersonal-skills/the-10-questions-you-need-to-be-a-better-listener/

Emma-Louise. (2013, June 28). *Relax Your Clients in Under 5 Minutes with these Guided Meditation Scripts | The Launchpad - The Coaching Tools Company Blog*. The Coaching Tools Company. https://www.thecoachingtoolscompany.com/de-stress-series-relax-clients-in-under-5-mins-guided-meditation-scripts/

Epictetus Quotes. (n.d.). BrainyQuote. https://www.brainyquote.com/quotes/epictetus_106298

Fletcher, J. (2016, May 17). *Guided Imagery: Relaxation Scripts for Meditation*. Psych Central. https://psychcentral.com/health/imagery-basic-relaxation-script#Relaxation-script-for-meditation

Forbes Coaches Council. (2016, May 4). 12 Techniques For Being Less Reactive And More Intentional With Workplace Communication. *Forbes*. https://www.forbes.com/sites/forbescoachescouncil/2016/05/04/12-techniques-to-be-less-reactive-and-more-intentional-with-workplace-communication/

George, J. (2024). Emotional Intelligence and the Importance of Communication for Introverts. LinkedIn Pulse. https://www.linkedin.com/pulse/emotional-intelligence-importance-communication-george-icf-pcc--rgcrc

George Bernard Shaw Quotes. (n.d.). BrainyQuote. https://www.brainyquote.com/quotes/george_bernard_shaw_385438

Gordon, S. (2020, June 27). *Everything You Need to Know About the Five Love Languages*. Verywell Mind. https://www.verywellmind.com/can-the-five-love-languages-help-your-relationship-4783538

Gupta, S. (2021, December 27). *How to Build Trust in a Relationship*. Verywell Mind. https://www.verywellmind.com/how-to-build-trust-in-a-relationship-5207611

Harandi, T. F., Taghinasab, M. M., & Nayeri, T. D. (2017). The Correlation of Social Support with Mental health: a meta-analysis. *Electronic Physician*, *9*(9), 5212–5222. https://doi.org/10.19082/5212

Harris, G. (2018, September 21). *That Escalated Quickly: 3 Words Guaranteed to Increase Conflict - The Kevin Eikenberry Group*. The Kevin Eikenberry Group. https://kevineikenberry.com/communication-interpersonal-skills/that-escalated-quickly-3-words-guaranteed-to-increase-conflict/

Hooper, L. (2018, November 21). *Transforming Conflict into Connection - Lydia Hooper - Medium*. Medium. https://lydiahooper.medium.com/transforming-conflict-into-connection-c83731e6f1b7

Horsager, D. (2014, July 3). *Conflict is Unavoidable | Trust in Relationships - David Horsager*. David Horsager. https://davidhorsager.com/conflict-is-unavoidable-trust-in-relationships/

Horton, L. (2019, August 8). *The Neuroscience Behind Our Words*. BRM Institute. https://brm.institute/neuroscience-behind-words/

How Do I Know If I'm Self-Aware? – The Friendly Mind. (2024). The Friendly Mind. https://www.thefriendlymind.com/how-do-i-know-if-im-self-aware/

How to be more empathetic: 8 exercises to develop empathy — Calm Blog. (2023, December 5). Calm Blog. https://www.calm.com/blog/how-to-be-more-empathetic

HRDQ Staff. (2022, August 16). *What Are Some Common Barriers to Effective Listening?* HRDQ Blog. https://hrdqstore.com/blogs/hrdq-blog/common-barriers-effective-listening

Janusik, L., & Rouillard, J. (n.d.). *Research Findings on Listening*. https://www.globallisteningcentre.org/wp-content/uploads/2020/07/research-findings-on-listening-laura-janusik.pdf

Johnny and June: a Country Music Love Story. (2023, August 2). Folsom Cash Art Trail. https://folsomcasharttrail.com/the-trail/blog/johnny-and-june-a-country-music-love-story

Joseph, M. (2023, July 21). *65 Relationship Check-In Questions to Keep You on the Same Page*. Thriving Good Life. https://thrivinggoodlife.com/relationship-check-in-questions/

Joseph Joubert Quotes. (n.d.). BrainyQuote. https://www.brainyquote.com/quotes/joseph_joubert_157297

Joyce Brothers Quotes. (n.d.). BrainyQuote. https://www.brainyquote.com/quotes/joyce_brothers_131256

Kaur, J., & Junnarkar, M. (2017). Emotional intelligence and intimacy in relationships. The International Journal of Indian Psychology, 4(3), 27-35. DOI: 10.25215/0403.084

Kessler, O. (2024a, May 11). *What Is the Role of Words in Relationships?* Marriage.com. https://www.marriage.com/advice/relationship/words-in-a-romantic-relationship/

Kessler, O. (2024b, May 21). *11 Things That Can Happen In Relationships Without Trust*. Marriage.com. https://www.marriage.com/advice/relationship/trust-issue-relationship-without-trust/

Krueger, A. (2019, May 26). *Trust Issues: Signs You Have Them and How to Get Over Them*. Brides. https://www.brides.com/story/signs-trust-issues-haunting-relationship

Kuppusamy, M., Kamaldeen, D., Pitani, R., Amaldas, J., & Shanmugam, P. (2018). Effects of Bhramari Pranayama on health – A systematic review. *Journal of Traditional and Complementary Medicine*, *8*(1), 11–16. https://doi.org/10.1016/j.jtcme.2017.02.003

Lack of Empathy: 8 Signs of Lack of Empathy. MasterClass. https://www.masterclass.com/articles/lack-of-empathy

Lebow, H. I. (2012, April 4). *Self-Soothing: 10 Ways to Calm Down and Find Balance*. Psych Central. https://psychcentral.com/anxiety/self-soothing-methods#self-soothing-techniques

Lebow, H. I. (2021, June 7). *How Can I Improve Emotional Intelligence (EQ)?* Psych Central. https://psychcentral.com/lib/what-is-emotional-intelligence-eq#why-its-important

Lisitsa, E. (2013). The Four Horsemen: Criticism, Contempt, Defensiveness, and Stonewalling. In *The Gottman Institute.* https://www.gottman.com/blog/the-four-horsemen-recognizing-criticism-contempt-defensiveness-and-stonewalling/

Lumia. (2023, August 10). *Build Self-Awareness: Ten Self-Reflection Exercises and Self-Assessment Tools | Lumia.* https://www.lumiacoaching.com/blog/self-awareness-tools

Mancao, A. (2022, March 11). *How to Communicate Your Feelings Effectively in a Relationship.* Theknot.com; The Knot. https://www.theknot.com/content/communicate-feelings

Mantell, M. (2022, March 15). *Vulnerability exercises to get more fulfilling relationships.* Mike Mantell. https://mikemantell.com/vulnerability-exercises/#3_vulnerability_exercises

Marriage.com Editorial Team. (2022, September 6). *15 Phrases That Will Diffuse Arguments With Your Partner.* Marriage.com. https://www.marriage.com/advice/relationship/how-to-diffuse-arguments-with-your-partner/

Martin, R. (2022, January 12). *50 tips for improving your emotional intelligence.* RocheMartin. https://www.rochemartin.com/blog/50-tips-improving-emotional-intelligence

Martins, J. (2022, October 27). *Listening to understand: How to practice active listening (with examples) • asana.* Asana. https://asana.com/resources/active-listening

MasterClass. (2020). *Accountability in Relationships: How to Practice Accountability.* MasterClass. https://www.masterclass.com/articles/accountability-in-relationships

McFadden, P. (2017, October 11). *3 Daily Rituals That Stop Spouses from Taking Each Other for Granted.* The Gottman Institute. https://www.gottman.com/blog/3-daily-rituals-that-stop-spouses-from-taking-each-other-for-granted/

Mignon McLaughlin Quotes. (n.d.). BrainyQuote. https://www.brainyquote.com/quotes/mignon_mclaughlin_125518

Morin, A. (2021, July 30). *11 Ways to Calm Yourself Fast When You're Really Mad.* Verywell Mind. https://www.verywellmind.com/anger-management-strategies-4178870

Morin, A. (2023, March 31). *Friday Fix: 10 Signs You Need Better Boundaries.* Verywell Mind. https://www.verywellmind.com/signs-you-need-better-boundaries-7373738

Nash, J. (2023, February 16). *Guided Imagery in Therapy: 20 Powerful Scripts and Techniques.* PositivePsychology. https://positivepsychology.com/guided-imagery-scripts/#activities

National University. (2018, November 20). *Seven Conflict Resolution Tips for Couples.* National University. https://www.nu.edu/blog/seven-conflict-resolution-tips-for-couples/

Oppland, M. (2017, April 28). *13 Most Popular Gratitude Exercises & Activities.* PositivePsychology. https://positivepsychology.com/gratitude-exercises/#exercises-gratitude

O'Bryan, A. (2021, December 4). *How to Perform Body Scan Meditation: 3 Best Scripts.* PositivePsychology. https://positivepsychology.com/body-scan-meditation/

O'Bryan, A. (2022, February 8). *How to Practice Active Listening: 16 Examples & Techniques.* PositivePsychology. https://positivepsychology.com/active-listening-techniques/#techniques

Pace, R. (2020, November 12). *16 Powerful Benefits of Vulnerability in Relationships*. Marriage.com. https://www.marriage.com/advice/relationship/benefits-of-vulnerability-in-relationships/

Pajer, N. (2021, May 12). *Navigating Different Communication Styles in Relationships*. Shondaland. https://www.shondaland.com/live/family/a36396758/navigating-different-communication-styles-in-relationships/

Palmer, M. (2023, November 7). *Types of Communication Styles And How to Identify Them*. Southern New Hampshire University. https://www.snhu.edu/about-us/newsroom/liberal-arts/types-of-communication-styles

Personality Disorders. Cleveland Clinic. https://my.clevelandclinic.org/health/diseases/9636-personality-disorders-overview

Powell, A. (2023). *50 Questions to Ask Your Partner to Increase Intimacy*. ChoosingTherapy. https://www.choosingtherapy.com/50-questions-to-ask-your-partner-to-increase-intimacy/

Practicing Pausing (STOP) - Wisdom & Wellbeing Program. (2024). Virginia. https://medicalcenter.virginia.edu/wwp/positive-practices-to-enhance-resilience-and-improve-interpersonal-communication-individual-techniques-1/self-regulation/practicing-pausing-stop/

Quote by Hafiz: "The words you speak become the house you live in." (2024). Goodreads. https://www.goodreads.com/quotes/85147-the-words-you-speak-become-the-house-you-live-in

Rahma, I. (2022, September 28). *How to Set Healthy Boundaries in Relationships*. Choosing Therapy. https://www.choosingtherapy.com/boundaries-in-relationships/

Ramsey, C. (2023, October 25). *Emotional Regulation: Everything You Need to Know to Improve Your Relationships.* Council for Relationships. https://councilforrelationships.org/emotional-regulation-everything-you-need-to-know-to-improve-your-relationships/

Raypole, C. (2024, January 29). *30 grounding techniques to quiet distressing thoughts*. Healthline. https://www.healthline.com/health/grounding-techniques

Reid, S. (2022, July 6). *Setting Healthy Boundaries in Relationships - HelpGuide.org*. HelpGuide. https://www.helpguide.org/relationships/social-connection/setting-healthy-boundaries-in-relationships

Reid, S. (n.d). Empathy: How to Feel and Respond to the Emotions of Others. HelpGuide. https://www.helpguide.org/relationships/communication/empathy

Rickardsson, J. (2024, September 24). *Stiftelsen 29k Foundation*. 29k.org. https://29k.org/article/5-reasons-why-empathy-is-important-in-relationships

Risser, M. (2022, September 15). *13 Signs of Trust Issues & How to Get Over Them*. Choosing Therapy. https://www.choosingtherapy.com/trust-issues/

Schewitz, S. (2023, December 4). *How to Build Trust in Relationships*. Couples Learn. https://coupleslearn.com/how-to-build-trust-in-relationships/

Scott, E. (2021, September 1). *5 Steps to Better Apology*. Verywell Mind. https://www.verywellmind.com/how-to-apologize-more-sincerely-3144467

Segal, J., Smith, M., & Robinson, L. (2024, August 21). *Improving Emotional Intelligence (EQ): Expert Guide*. HelpGuide. https://www.helpguide.org/mental-health/wellbeing/emotional-intelligence-eq

Segal, J., Smith, M. and Robinson, L. (n.d). Improving Emotional Intelligence (EQ): Manage Emotions to Build Better Relationships and Achieve Success. HelpGuide. https://www.helpguide.org/mental-health/wellbeing/emotional-intelligence-eq

Segal, J. (n.d). How to Be Emotionally Intelligent in Romantic Relationships. HelpGuide. https://www.helpguide.org/mental-health/wellbeing/emotional-intelligence-love-relationships

Smith, G. (2020, August 20). *How to Be Vulnerable in a Relationship: Tips for Deeper Connection*. Greatist. https://greatist.com/connect/vulnerability-in-relationships#encouraging-your-partner-to-open-up

Starfire, A. L. (2011, March 21). *A Week's Worth of Journaling Prompts: Vulnerability – Writing Through Life*. Writing through Life. https://writingthroughlife.com/a-weeks-worth-of-journaling-prompts-vulnerability/

Stritof, S. (2018). *Tips for Rebuilding Trust in Your Marriage*. Verywell Mind. https://www.verywellmind.com/rebuild-trust-in-your-marriage-2300999

Taylor, C. (n.d.). *Ten Steps for Resolving Couple Conflict Worksheet*. Retrieved November 21, 2024, from https://camtaylor.net/wp-content/uploads/2012/12/10-steps-for-resolving-conflict-general.pdf

Team, B. E. (2019, June 18). *Rekindling The Spark in Your Relationship | BetterHelp*. BetterHelp. https://www.betterhelp.com/advice/love/rekindling-the-spark-how-to-fall-back-in-love/

The Break. (2014). Alano Club of Portland. https://www.portlandalano.org/the-break

The importance of intimacy in a relationship - Positivity Guides. (2023, September 29). Positivity Guides. https://www.positivityguides.net/intimacy-in-a-relationship

The Power of Patience ~ The Emotions Series - Intentional Communication Consultants. (2018, May 9). Intentional Communication Consultants. https://intentionalcommunication.com/the-emotions-series-the-power-of-patience/

THE SCIENCE OF ACTIVE LISTENING. (2023, March 2). Jim Kwik. https://www.jimkwik.com/the-science-of-active-listening/

These 10 Qualities Make You An Exceptional Listener. (2021, December 4). MindDoc. https://minddoc.de/magazin/en/exceptional-listener/

The Self-Awareness Guy. (2023, February 10). *Self-Awareness and Effective Communication – Tips to Improve Self-Awareness*. The Self-Awareness Guy. https://www.theselfawarenessguy.com/4573/self-awareness-and-effective-communication

Things You Should Never Say To Your Partner - Dig Counseling Services. (2022, July 20). Dig Counseling Services. https://digcounseling.com/8-things-you-should-never-say-to-your-partner/

Thompson, T. (2017, July 24). *Validation Do's and Don'ts for Couples: An Essential Component to Finally Feeling Understood!* Your Life. Your Story. Your Journey. https://tthompsontherapy.blog/2017/07/24/validation-dos-and-donts-for-couples-an-essential-component-to-finally-feeling-understood/

Thueson, A. (2023, April 7). *30-Day Love Challenge – Be Extra in Your Relationship - Andie Thueson*. Andie Thueson. https://andiethueson.com/30-day-love-challenge/

Trivedi, G. Y., Sharma, K., Saboo, B., Kathirvel, S., Konat, A., Zapadia, V., Prajapati, P. J., Benani, U., Patel, K., & Shah, S. (2023). Humming (Simple Bhramari Pranayama) as a Stress Buster: A Holter-Based Study to Analyze Heart Rate Variability (HRV) Parameters During Bhramari, Physical Activity, Emotional Stress, and Sleep. *Cureus*. https://doi.org/10.7759/cureus.37527

UAGC Staff Member. (2021, December 10). *The psychology behind the 5 love languages*. The University of Arizona Global Campus. https://www.uagc.edu/blog/the-psychology-behind-the-5-love-languages

University of Minnesota. (2016). *5.2 Barriers to Effective Listening*. LIBRARIES; University of Minnesota Libraries Publishing. https://open.lib.umn.edu/communication/chapter/5-2-barriers-to-effective-listening/

Waldman, L. F. (2019, June 11). *Five Ways to Argue Constructively with Your Partner*. Find a Psychologist. https://www.findapsychologist.org/five-ways-to-argue-constructively-with-your-partner-by-dr-larry-f-waldman/

What Makes a Good Relationship? Gratitude, Say Experts. (2022, February 1). Health Concepts. https://healthconceptsltd.com/2022/02/01/what-makes-a-good-relationship-gratitude-say-experts/

Wilshiere, J. (2021, October 8). *The Importance of Listening Skills in Communication*. One Education. https://www.oneeducation.org.uk/importance-of-listening-skills-in-communication/

Zimmerman, C. (2024, April 24). *Master Communication Styles in Relationships!* Counseling Associates for Well-Being. https://ca4wellbeing.com/communication-styles-in-relationships/

Made in United States
Orlando, FL
18 March 2025

59574868R00102